following AMELIA

A Modern-Day 'Round-the-World Flight

By Sandi Smith

Wishing you soaring success!

Sandi Smith

Ruby MOON PRESS

Irving, Texas

Published by:
Ruby Moon Press
3817 Yellowstone
Irving, TX 75062

Web: http://www.followingamelia.com

http://www.rubymoonpress.com

EDUCATIONAL AND INFORMATIONAL PURPOSES ONLY

This book is provided for educational and informational purposes only and does not provide professional advice or service. Use of any information in the book does not create a professional relationship with Sandra L. Smith, P.C. You should not act on the information provided in this product without seeking additional professional counsel.

ISBN 0-9665370-1-7

Printed in the United States of America

Designed by Matt Mitchell

To all the people we met on the trip;
may all your dreams come true.

To all the women who fly or who want to;
may all your ambitions be realized.

Acknowledgements

I have dozens of people to thank. First, there is Jay Merten. Without his unquenchable ambition, this trip would never have been attempted.

Next there was our cheerleading home team in Dallas, Texas and Monroe, Louisiana: my mom and dad, Jay's mom and dad, Ed and Lia, Steve, Ernie, and many more.

Thanks to all of the professionals who contributed to the success of the trip: Sharon Fries of Jeppesen, Donn Kerby and all the people Jay talked to before the trip, the people at India International Airways, Osman, and Trevor of Phoenix Aviation. I am grateful to all who helped us accomplish this flight.

I'd like to acknowledge the wonderful people at the Lumbini Rana-Ambika Eye Hospital, the Kathmandu Seva office, and the Berkeley Seva office. Dr. Dhital, Chitra Karn, Ganesh, Meena, Mr. Dhakhwa, Suzanne, Alexa, and so many more. I am humble and grateful for your extraordinary service to mankind. Thank you for what you do and for making us feel so welcome in a sea of strangers.

I'd also like to acknowledge the people at the Lighthouse for Christ Eye Center. Thank you for your hospitality and warmth. You weren't certain about me at the beginning, but you embraced me nevertheless. Frank, Phyllis, Onesman, Nora, Doreen, Gary, Jean, Roberta, Thula, Francesca, and many more, I appreciate your faith.

My personal appreciation goes to my writing community. Especially: LaRee Bryant, who made this book tons better than I thought it ever could be, Deborah Morris, who painstakingly line-edited a chapter to get me on the right track, and Melody Stanford, who contributed her extensive fiction experience to making an early draft better. My gratitude goes to all the writers at Tejas for listening to me at our lunches, and for the people close to me who missed a movie or two so that I could write.

Table of Contents

Introduction

"When you are inspired by some great purpose, some extraordinary project, all your thoughts break their bonds."

-Patanjali

Jay Merten and I had been dating for a couple of years when he popped the question. (No, not that question.)

"Want to take the Malibu around the world?"

Few women get asked to fly a small, private airplane around the world. My research shows that only five other American women have taken a trip such as this one. Worldwide, the number increases to less than twenty. Unfortunately, we can't count the famous female aviator Amelia Earhart as one of those women. She and her navigator, Fred Noonan, perished in the Pacific in their 1937 attempt to circumnavigate the world after missing their target, Howland Island. In 1949, the first woman who circled the earth was Britain's Richarda Morrow-Tait, and she flew with two navigators in a single engine airplane. American Geraldine Mock managed the first solo circumnavigation in a single engine Cessna 180 in 1964.

Statistically, the odds are one in 150 million for a woman to complete a circumnavigation in a small airplane. That's rarer than winning most state lotteries. How could I possibly say no to a one-in-150-million-lifetimes question?

I accepted the challenge.

My answer came partly out of the answer to this question:

"Will I regret it if I pass this opportunity up?" Yes, I would regret it, and I knew the opportunity, as rare as it was, would never arise again in my lifetime. You only have one chance at opportunities like these.

My "yes" came partly as a result of my passion for traveling. I adore traveling. I love arriving in a strange place with no idea where I'm going to stay or eat or sightsee, then spending all day exploring and finding what I need. I love meeting people who are very different from me and finding out what makes them tick. What habits do they have that I might want to bring into my own life to make it better? This trip would allow me to see over a dozen new countries and their cultures.

My "yes" also came as a result of my trust in Jay's piloting skills. He is so passionate about flying that he reads the NTSB (National Transportation Safety Board) accident reports regularly, studies what happened, and modifies his own flying procedures to be safer. I felt safe with him and confident of his mastery of flying.

My "yes" came after careful deliberation of the risks we would face on the trip. We calculated that we had, roughly, a one percent chance of dying before we completed our adventure. Saying yes to an extraordinary project like this one requires a belief that you will be successful despite the odds. And, most importantly, that if you fail, you'll suffer the consequences of failure, without regret, even if it's death. I also knew that we would reduce the risks as much as possible by preparing for them. We would think through scenarios that could occur and be ready for them. Engine failure, fire, ditching into the sea, equipment breakdowns, political issues, weather extremes, forced landings; we would be prepared for all of these possibilities.

But most of all, my "yes" resulted because of a pet peeve

I have about the human race. I believe people live too small. We get too comfortable on our couches in front of TV shows, the Internet, or video games. We watch and read about other people who do great things but never dare to do any of that for ourselves.

If some catastrophe befalls us, we rise to the occasion or perish. People survive cancer, fires, attacks and other horrible things because they *have* to. I'm not wishing those things on anyone, of course. But when a crisis comes calling, you live at whatever higher level you need to in order to survive the crisis. You live bigger than you ever thought you could. You do whatever it takes.

About her dream, Amelia Earhart said, "I flew the Atlantic because I wanted to. To want in one's head to do a thing, for its own sake; to enjoy doing it; to concentrate all of one's energies upon it - that is not only the surest guarantee of its success. It is also being true to oneself."

What if our lives are great? Plain, but great? Great job, great kids, great house, great spouse? It's really hard to challenge yourself to live at the next level if everything is going well in your life. But that's what Jay was asking me to do.

And I was ready.

July 6, 1995
Portland, Maine, USA

"When once you have tasted flight you will forever walk the earth with your eyes turned skyward."

—Leonardo da Vinci

*B*uckled in the copilot's seat of Jay Merten's 1987 Piper Malibu, I shiver from the predawn cold and from sheer fear. Sitting to my left, Jay listens to the radio broadcast and balances a clipboard on his lap. Holding a flashlight in one hand and a pen in the other, he scribbles several numbers on a piece of paper. Bangor Center has just radioed the details of our air traffic control clearance information.

"I got the squawk code," I report. I dial in the radar identification and recheck the radio frequencies on the panel.

"OK. Stow this for me, please," Jay says. He hands the clipboard to me and grips the yoke.

Today's flight will be a long one, even if all goes well. I

wriggle to get comfortable in my seat. With only a few hours of anxious sleep last night, I can tell I'm going to be more fidgety than normal this flight. I'm not what you would call a morning person; it's one of my biggest weaknesses. Only the excitement and fear of this moment is keeping me from closing my eyes and zoning into a snooze. Outside the cockpit window, a heavy fog encases the airport taxiways and runways. The smell of gas overwhelms the normally pleasant leathery smell inside the airplane. The engine is humming, the brakes are holding, and the little plane's solitary propeller is pointed into the wind. We are in position to depart on the airport runway, and at any minute we'll be cleared for takeoff.

We've been up many times before. This time, though, we're not sure the little gray and maroon airplane is going to get off the ground with all the fuel it's carrying for our long over-water flight.

Jay is noticeably tense, not something you want to see in your airplane pilot. With penetrating blue eyes and frowning gray brows behind dark plastic-rimmed glasses, he focuses on the moment's task. His complexion is pale; his face thin. His 5'10," 163-pound torso fits easily into the beige leather cockpit seat. A black Bowes headset fits snugly over his ears. I wear a headset, too. We can't hear each other's voices directly; we can only communicate through the radio system. This early in the morning, I'm not much of a talker, which is perfect because Jay has much to concentrate on.

Yesterday, a maintenance worker added a makeshift metal fuel tank right behind my seat so we'd have enough fuel to cross the two oceans. Welded at its seams, the new 120-gallon auxiliary tank doubles our fuel capacity. It sits on a couple of pieces of plywood, and a plastic tube exits the tank at the bottom and runs between Jay's and my seat. The tube is attached to a two-by-four with a couple of metal fasteners. A lever controls the tube's fuel flow. I wouldn't be surprised if there were some band-aids and bubblegum on this homemade-looking contraption. We're betting our lives on this pitiful-looking invention.

The new tank is brimming with avgas (aviation gasoline), and fumes saturate the cockpit, even though the tank is tightly capped. The request "no smoking, please" implies life-and-death consequences. Even a wayward spark could create an explosive fire. The smell is no fun, but I don't feel sick from it.

The plane's two permanent fuel tanks are located in each wing. Over gross weight by 25 percent because of the extra fuel, the plane's compressed main gear and flattened tires struggle to hold up its weight. In the last few days, every scrap of luggage has been weighed, double-checked, and added to the weight and balance computation to make sure the plane is still airworthy. The plane's center of gravity had to be calculated as well. Jay and I also stepped on the scale, and, ladies, this is no time to lie about your weight. It isn't every day that your life depends upon the answer to a math problem.

Usually I like numbers. I seem to be drawn to professions that use math: accounting and computers. A practical, earthy type, I even look a little geeky. My blue eyes do not need geeky glasses, however. I'm pretty proud of that. With an olive complexion, I tan easily. My short brown hair, still damp from this morning's wash, curls naturally when I let it air dry. I'm 5'3 ½", 106 pounds, a comfortable size four petite.

Our destination is a beautiful set of remote islands in the eastern Atlantic Ocean called the Azores, a Portuguese territory. Today's trip is only one leg of a longer journey, a trip around the world, from Dallas, Texas, USA, eastbound to Dallas, Texas, USA. The previous week we departed Dallas and landed in Monroe, Louisiana to visit family; Virginia Beach to see old friends; Hampton, Virginia to visit a former home; and Portland, Maine to install the extra equipment for this flight. Our adventure will transport us to foreign lands, over seemingly unending stretches of oceans, deserts, and mountains, and through unfamiliar weather patterns with challenges such as monsoons, typhoons, stifling heat, and extreme density altitude readings. Pilots call a voyage like this a circumnavigation of the earth in light aircraft. Jay calls it the dream of his lifetime. I am not sure *what* to call it. I only know that I am passionate about traveling, I trust Jay's piloting skills, and I'm absolutely certain the chance won't come around again.

This early morning, it's dark and foggy with only an eighth of a mile visibility. Two hazy orange lines of lights outline the edges of the runway in front of us. A white glow of lights illuminates the center line. The airport buildings line the runway on the left side. There is no room for error. If something bad happens during takeoff, the foggy condition will preclude us from being able to turn around and land again.

Will we be able to get off the ground? Will the plane fly with its extra payload? Will we make it across the ocean without the lone engine giving out?

The stakes are high. Several pilots in similar situations have lost their lives. On May 21st, just weeks ago, a pilot flying a Cessna from Gander, Newfoundland to Vienna, Austria ran into trouble off the coast of Portugal. He reported to air traffic controllers that he had no fuel and that both engines had stopped. In 60-knot winds, the seas were rough. That was the last they heard from him. Searchers found safety and flotation equipment from the aircraft, but the plane and the pilot were never found.

In October 1993, a helicopter pilot was caught in bad weather while trying to land on an offshore platform. Flying too low, the craft was struck by a 15-foot swell and rolled into the ocean. The two passengers escaped by swimming to the platform, but the pilot wasn't so lucky. Unconscious, he was floating face down in the water. When rescuers attempted to recover him, his life jacket slipped off and he sank to his death.

Even the Navy can have bad days at sea. In March, a P-3C Orion was forced to ditch when all *four* of its engines failed during a routine patrol in the Gulf of Oman. All crew were rescued safely, however.

In 1928, Amelia Earhart became the first woman passenger to fly across the Atlantic. During the flight of the Friendship, she never touched the controls. Pilot Wilmer Stultz and mechanic Louis Gordon did all the aviation work on the famous flight. Amelia felt funny for receiving so much publicity for basically doing nothing. Four years later, she vindicated herself by piloting her Vega from North America to Ireland and becoming the first woman to solo across the Atlantic Ocean.

In the dark cockpit, Jay gently requests, "I need you to call out the indicated air speeds during takeoff. Will you set the power for takeoff?"

"OK." I move the power lever, and Jay advances the throttle at the same time.

For days now, Jay has been very nervous about this takeoff. Months of planning and years of experience will be tested in the next few seconds. Our success or failure will be determined by how well we thought through the scenarios that could happen to us and how well we prepared for them.

There are so many risks on a flight like this. The key to success is to first try to prevent them from happening. But you can't just stop there. You have to also be ready if they do happen. You have to be ready in such an automatic way that your training and instincts kick in instead of your emotions. And that means lots of practice and mastery.

"Here we go." He lifts his feet off the brakes. Jay is all business, more so than normal. Adrenaline floods my body as the engine's drone intensifies and we start to roll. Jay makes the remaining takeoff adjustments swiftly.

Over the 25 years he has been flying, Jay has advanced from private pilot license to instrument-rated to a commercial license. Four months ago, just before he turned 48, Jay earned his ATP: Airline Transport Pilot. Now he has over 1,500 flying hours logged.

The Malibu lumbers like an elephant down the runway. I assume my duties. "Air speed alive... 40... 50..."

The plane is more sluggish than I have ever experienced. Jay selected this extra-long runway to allow more room for error. With rock-solid concentration, he glances at the gauges and peers ahead through the cockpit windscreen into the foggy darkness. He manipulates the rudder pedals to keep the plane going perfectly straight, tracing the white center line of the runway.

"60...70..."

I catch a glimpse of a runway marker in my peripheral vision. I quickly sneak a look to see how much runway we have left. A tall cluster of trees stands amid the fog at the end of the runway ahead of us.

"80..."

Finally we reach the speed at which you pull the yoke back. It's now or never for the Malibu.

"Rotate!"

Jay pulls the yoke toward him with one hand; his other hand is on the throttle. The wheels and the pavement separate; the nose rises into the sky.

Below, the runway lights disappear abruptly, and fog surrounds us. We are in the air, climbing ever so gradually. Jay's nervousness turns into controlled elation.

I know Jay is thrilled to be doing this flight, his life dream. I believe he is also grateful that I agreed to be his copilot. I don't think he would be able to do this flight without a partner, and I'm honored to have been asked. Our partnership is quite synergistic, both personally and in the air as a flight crew.

"So far so good. After-takeoff checklist," Jay calls.

I retrieve the sheet of paper from the pocket on the wall near the breakers. "Gear," I read.

"Up," Jay answers.

"Flaps."

"Up."

"Yaw damper."

"On."

"Climb power."

"Set."

"After takeoff checklist complete."

"I'm really glad that went well. It wouldn't have been easy aborting in that heavy of fog," Jay reports.

"Me, too. Good job, Captain," I add. I'm limp with relief that we've passed this first milestone on our flight. But the trip has just started, and we have many more challenges ahead of us today, not to mention for the rest of the journey. I'm apprehensive, and also a little sleepy. The ascent, like the takeoff, is slothful. Jay engages the autopilot, which flies the airplane more than either of us.

The fog dissipates as we climb steadily. The cockpit is

warmer now than when we started out. This is good since I've always been a little cold-natured. Jay keeps warm in his khakis, a maroon short-sleeved polo shirt, and a light jacket. He's always tastefully dressed. I dress for comfort: blue jeans and a white long-sleeved sweatshirt that I bought in Amsterdam years ago. We can control the temperature of the cockpit with the heater and air conditioner, so it's always comfortable.

Jay turns off the flashlight. "Look at the stars."

As our eyes adjust to the darkness, the stars multiply in the sky. The more we stare into the dark, the more stars we see. Just beyond the windscreen, thousands and thousands of them shine in all shades of brightness in every direction we look. There are exponentially more stars in view now than I've ever seen while camping or boating.

"Beautiful," I reply. "Look at the sunrise. I think it will be faster than normal this morning." Straight ahead, out of the blackness, a wafer thin orange halo rests above the horizon. Going eastbound, time will advance quicker and the sun will rise faster. Or so it will seem from our vantage point.

The peaceful hum of the engine is the sole sound for miles. The magnificence of the predawn scene steals my breath. Few people experience a sight like this from above the earth. Both Jay and I gawk at the beauty in silence.

Jay, more animated now that the takeoff is behind us, loves every minute of flying. It's been his passion since he discovered the "A" encyclopedia as a boy: Aerodynamics, Air Force, Airplanes, Aviation. Buying the Malibu four years ago was one of his most exciting moments.

Pop!! A sharp gunshot sound in the cabin suddenly pierces the stillness.

I jump, then I immediately start troubleshooting.

Jay instinctively does the same. He examines the cockpit

and summarizes his thoughts. "We didn't just blow up, so that's good news. The wings are still attached, so that's good news," he declares, quickly inspecting all the gauges. Everything registers in normal range. "Why don't you look in back?" Jay suggests.

"OK." I unbuckle my harness and creep out of my seat to investigate. The cabin is not tall enough for me to stand up, so I have to hunch over as I climb around in back. The air reeks of gasoline fumes as I glance around.

The first thing I scrutinize is the cabin door. The door's handle is set to the locked position, a normal indication. "Cabin door is normal," I call out. The beige carpet and the four passenger seats have been removed to make the craft as light as possible, so the cabin appears different in comparison to what I am used to. The emergency equipment consumes quite a bit of space and weight. The life raft alone weighs 80 pounds.

Jay receives a radio call. "Come on back, I need you up here," he says.

Sheesh. I'm not finished searching yet, I think to myself. At that moment, I spot the gas tank top lying on the floor. It popped off like a cork released from a champagne bottle as the air in the cabin depressurized and the air in the tank remained at sea level. I pick up the top and place it loosely back on so the tank can breathe. It isn't going to get any stinkier, so there's no need to tightly cap the tank. Mystery solved, I crawl back to my seat and buckle up. When he gets off the radio, I tell Jay the news.

"Oh, good," he says, relieved to hear that the strange sound means nothing. "Let's check the waypoint on the GPS," he decides. GPS stands for Global Positioning System. It contains a database of all of the points that are found on routes of flight all around the world. The built-in GPS computer is really cool; I can track our flight path, locate the nearest airport, find out how much fuel is used, tell how fast we're going, know how high we are, and look up how many miles and minutes are left before we land. There is no keyboard, just a couple of knobs and several fast-function buttons. You have to learn how to set the knobs to the various functions, which causes different screens to display, but once you do that, it's easy to control. To enter data, you punch the cursor button and rotate the knob to the correct lever. I locate the checkpoint on the chart that I have unfolded in my lap. Jay channel-surfs the green-on-black GPS screens.

The flight plan traces the Canadian coastline for about 400 miles. After that, the topography will change from land to ocean, thousands of miles of it. The nearest airport will be too far away if we have a problem in the middle of the Atlantic. For some reason, I am only mildly anxious, even somewhat calm, about this. Perhaps my mind thinks nothing can possibly happen to us (even though we've prepared otherwise) now that we're airborne. Perhaps this is how the brain conserves energy for when you really need it.

To reach the Azores, we'll fly more than 2,000 nautical miles today. One nautical mile equals 1.15 statute, or regular, miles. We'll be up in the air for eleven hours, averaging a speed of 180 knots (nautical miles per hour).

Inside the cockpit, the black instrument panel glows orange and white with displays, gauges, radio frequencies, and various switches. Each gauge - the air speed indicator, attitude indicator, altimeter, turn coordinator, compass, vertical speed indicator, and engine gauges such as the manifold pressure, the RPM, and the oil temperature - displays a normal position that you hope for when you look at it. It's good practice to do a "sweep" of the gauges every twenty seconds or so. It might sound boring to repeat the same task every twenty seconds, but doing exactly this greatly reduces the risk we take in flight. If we stay on top of things, we can catch them early and respond to them promptly before they get out of hand and become more dangerous. Noticing little things early is part of mastering the skill of flying.

One gauge catches my eye. "The cylinder head temperature gauge is a hair from redline," I say calmly, although I am not feeling calm. This gauge tells a pilot whether the engine is overheating. It's not the first time I've seen this reading.

Jay has already noticed it. "Got it," he says, not nearly as worried as I am. In the Malibu, the engine tends to run hot due to a design flaw in the airplane's air flow. This puts limitations on the airplane's ability to perform in more demanding conditions, such as a steep climb, extremely hot weather conditions, or high-altitude takeoffs and landings. To keep the gauge from registering any hotter, Jay "leans" the mixture of fuel, which reduces the amount flowing to the engine. He's worked around this issue ever since he's owned the plane.

Above the gauges on the instrument panel, the warning lights shine green, yellow and orange, depending on the severity of the problem. Luckily, none are shining now. To the right of the warning lights is the radio stack, which holds multiple radios in case of failure. It's lined up in the middle between the pilot's and copilot's seats. Orange numbers digitally display the radio frequencies that we're currently tuned to. The high frequency radio box sits on top of the fuel tank behind my seat. It's not mounted into the panel since it's an add-on for this trip. We need it to communicate long-distance across the oceans with air traffic control. All over the instrument panel are switches that control features such as the de-icing system, the yaw damper, the running lights, and much more. Having redundant gauges helps to reduce the risks and consequences of equipment failure. For such a small plane, the Malibu is loaded with equipment.

The sun's orange halo has transformed into its normal red ball and is slowly rising straight ahead of us in the clear blue sky.

"That was a fantastic sunrise," Jay says. "We can stow the flashlights now."

"I can start scanning for traffic," I add, squinting a little at the glare. It isn't as busy up here as it is on the Interstate.

"Most of the traffic will be 200 to 300 miles north, where the commercial jets are tracking the great circle route between the United States and Europe," Jay notes.

After a couple of hours of flying, I lean forward to gaze out the windshield. The sapphire waters stretch for miles in every direction. We'll be out here for hours. Ahead, bright puffs of cumulus clouds form an unbroken line that extends along the horizon. Over the ocean, with no land to disturb it, the cold front is perfect. It's as if Martha Stewart took a giant cake decorating kit and squirted out these dense round cumulus spheres in perfect uniformity.

"Do you see that front?" Jay asks, referring to the line of clouds ahead.

"Yep."

"That line is solid. There is no way to fly over it or around it. We'll have to navigate through it," concludes Jay.

The thought is bothersome. Inside the beautiful billows lurk thunderstorms... and ice.

The worst part is we have 60 nautical miles to think about it before we reach it.

Just before we left at 4:00 a.m., Jay checked the weather forecast and the skies were clear for most of the ocean flying. Since this flight is several hours long, weather systems can develop and change in route. You can obtain a weather update while you're flying by asking the controllers, but we've done this only for the most severe of weather systems.

In flying, fatal errors usually occur when more than one thing goes wrong at the same time. Call it the "three strikes and you're out" rule. Usually you can get away with doing one or even two stupid things at a time. When you do three stupid things at once, or if three unlucky things happen at the same time, that's when most aviation accidents occur. The equipment, the terrain, and the weather are the factors with which pilots must match wits on every flight. Pilot error is what causes most accidents, and a person is over 100 times more likely to die in a little plane than on a commercial flight.

On this flight, we have one or two strikes against us right out of the chute. The new fuel tank is "strike one." The flight path over the frigid Atlantic is "strike two." I try not to think about the things that could become "strike three."

6 July, 1995
Atlantic Ocean

"I do not think that a flight across the Atlantic will be made in our time, and in our time, I include the youngest readers."

—Charles Stewart Rolls
Co-founder of Rolls-Royce, Inc.
c.1908

*B*efore we left on this trip, I tried to learn as much about flying as time would allow. I completed a classroom course and aced the written exam for a private pilot's license. The license requires 15 to 20 hours of flight instruction, a solo flight, and a check ride. I received about eight hours of instruction from Rebecca, a young, cute flight instructor in a green two-seat Cessna 150 nicknamed the Gremlin. Then time ran out. I never soloed. The thought of soloing scares me to death. After all, you risk your life every time you get in the plane. I often wonder if I have the personality to assume the heavy responsibilities of a pilot. I think I make a pretty good copilot, but that may be as far as I can go. Still, I figured the more I could learn about flying, the less risk I would be taking on this trip. Now over the Atlantic, every skill I have is coming in handy.

"Want to fly it?" Jay asks.

"Sure." I grasp the yoke, gaze ahead at the horizon, peek at the altimeter from the corner of my eye, and fly the airplane straight and level.

As we approach the menacing clouds, Jay studies the possible routes we can take based on the radar picture. The weather radar displays red cells straight ahead of us. Of the three levels of precipitation, green, yellow, and red, red represents the most severe activity. You can't always predict what's happening in the cloud's interior until you actually fly inside, but it can include rain, wind, ice, hail, and unstable air.

"Not too many good options here," Jay says. "It's going to be bumpy."

"Doesn't look like much green to choose from," I reply, referring to the radar colors. "You're going to have to maneuver in the yellow areas."

"Just so we stay out of the red." Jay selects a path between two storm cells on the radar screen. He activates the anti-ice system. This heats the propeller and warms a hot plate in the windscreen. Each wing is equipped with de-icing boots. Jay takes over the flying, and we dart into the clouds with a bump.

"Will you watch for ice, please?" Jay asks.

"Will do," I roger.

The whiteness swallows us, as if we're in a dense fog or even a blizzard. With no visual clues through the windscreen, it's as if I've lost one of my five senses. Up looks like down, and down looks like up. To avoid disorientation, a pilot must switch her perspective from watching the horizon to watching the instruments. Flying IMC (instrument meteorological conditions) demands an instrument rating, training and certification that Jay has and I don't.

The turbulence jolts me in my seat. The little gray Malibu is at the mercy of the winds, the lightning, and the instability that occur inside the cloud formations. Wind shear can drop the plane several hundred feet at once. Over the Gulf of Mexico last year, in a tall cumulus buildup, we hit a wind shift that dropped the plane so fast it caused Jay to bump his head on the cockpit ceiling. Right now I feel pretty helpless, but I shift my energy to monitoring Jay's navigational choices and following the GPS.

There is just enough visibility for me to watch the wings and the high frequency radio antenna for signs of ice, as Jay requested. He manages to keep a steady grip on the yoke. He tightens his seat harness. I inspect mine. It's scary for both of us. Weather is one of the top causes of crashes.

"A little ice is sticking to the antenna," I report. "But not enough to be a problem." The high frequency radio antenna outside the airplane is the first thing that will attract ice since it's so thin. Jay glances over and nods his head in acknowledgement. The buildup is minimal but gradual. As turbulence jostles our bodies around in our seats, Jay's hand unsteadily grabs at a knob on the panel to adjust the scale of the radar. More ice forms on the leading edge of the wing.

We fly bumpily along in the opacity for a good twenty minutes. It might be common to be afraid of turbulence, but it's not logical. In light turbulence, most people naturally think that the plane could stop flying and start falling out of the sky. But light turbulence will not suddenly cause the plane to stop flying. As long as the plane is not thrown into a position where the pilots cannot recover, light turbulence is nothing to be afraid of. But clouds are. And turbulence just happens to go with them.

Sometimes in the clouds, my body feels lightheaded and nauseous, but today I'm just frightened. When will this feeling of helplessness be over? The radar displays red cells all around. How many miles wide is this storm? I practice my routine of reviewing gauges and studying charts to keep myself occupied and to try to stay calm. Then the turbulence increases. Nerves frayed, I catch another good jerk in the seat.

Suddenly we fly out of the white and into the blue. The bumps stop, and the ride is smooth. My body melts into my seat as I relax. I'm relieved to be able to see the earth again, even though it is the deep blue sea, and not land, below.

"The captain has turned off the seat belt sign. You may now move about the cabin. We should be in for a smooth ride," I joke. Jay smiles. Of course, as crew, we have our seat belts on the whole trip.

The drone of the engine is sure and steady amid the occasional crackle of the radio. The sun is now high in the sky. Ahead, the cloudless sky and the Atlantic Ocean, one shade deeper than the sky, form a backdrop of cobalt out the window of the tiny plane. It's a good thing my favorite color is blue.

"We've reached the point of no return," Jay says, scanning the GPS about six hours into the flight. "We have enough fuel to go back to Portland and call this whole thing off if we want to."

"You want to quit?" I kid him.

"I don't want to turn back," he replies. "Do you?"

"Of course not." I'm up for the adventure. I really respect Jay's expertise. He has the drive to be excellent at everything he does, and I like that in a man.

To further develop the special flying skills needed for this trip, Jay met with as many people as he could find who had experience with ocean flying or circumnavigations. Donn Kerby's name had come to the top of the list. A seasoned ferry pilot, one who transports new airplanes from the manufacturer to the owner, Donn prepared a two-inch thick orange binder of notes on the trip for us. The information in the binder was invaluable in determining the route we would fly, the budget to expect, and the problems to anticipate. In May and June, Jay and I spent our date nights studying these and other aviation materials instead of going to the movies. Jay also spoke at length with Ross Bowie, a Canadian who flew a 60-day round-the-world trip in a Malibu. Ross is an official of Transport Canada, a government agency that is similar to the US's FAA.

Jay found about a dozen other people who had flown around the world. He discovered them through magazine articles and pilot associations. He was able to discuss our round-the-world plans with many of them and to listen to their advice. In all, there are probably only a few hundred other people in the entire world who have attempted a trip such as this one. With such a tiny population, Jay was lucky to find so many experienced ocean and round-the-world pilots to talk with.

Before the start of this trip, Jay and two of his buddies from his high school days crossed the North Atlantic twice in the Malibu. In 1993, he flew the Malibu from Canada to France for the Paris Air Show via Iceland, the Faroe Islands, Norway, and Germany. Westbound, he returned via Belgium, Ireland, Scotland, Greenland, and Saint-Pierre et Miquelon off Newfoundland. In preparation for those travels, Jay took a North Atlantic Flight Planning Orientation

Course in New Hampshire from a company called Export Aircraft.

We both studied terrific books on overseas flying - Beryl Markham's *West with the Night* and Louise Sacchi's *Ocean Flying*. Jay read *East African Weather for Aviators*, a Kenyan publication by Mike Mwebesa. For some unexplainable reason, I was drawn to literature about Amelia Earhart.

Because of her time in history, Amelia Earhart took many more risks than today's aviators do on a circumnavigation. Her plane, the Lockheed-10 Electra, was a twin engine monoplane that held 10 passengers. It was designed for short hops and not at all for long-distance flying. Like us, Amelia had to take out the seats in order to accommodate the extra fuel tanks she'd need for ocean flying. In her case, she needed six extra tanks, not just one. The plane's fuselage had to be strengthened to carry the extra weight. The equipment, the navigational tools, and the weather forecasts were all less precise, to say the least, than they are today. Amelia was a risk-taker and, in her words, "liked danger."

Jay and I know the risks we're taking on our flight. We've tried our best to manage them wisely, and we're willing to see it out until the end. The studying, preparation, and practice will all contribute to the success or failure of the trip. Staying alive depends on Jay's flying experience and our planning.

While the plane consumes fuel, we equalize the amount of remaining avgas in each wing so that the plane's weight will be properly distributed. The engine can consume fuel from only one wing tank at a time. The cabin tank's fuel must drain into one of the wings before it can be used. Jay adjusts a lever to begin draining gas from the cabin tank into the left wing tank. In a detailed log of fuel usage by tank, we record each of these transfers and the number of gallons used. Despite both of us being analytical types, we devised an extremely unscientific but very workable approach to periodically checking the remaining fuel quantity in the new gas tank. I procure a flashlight and a hand mirror, rotate in my seat, hold the hand mirror up to the tank's small opening, and guess the level by the amount of sloshing going on.

I proceed to test our methodology.

Jay bellows, "Don't drop the flashlight into the tank."

I reply, "Okay, I'll try." The words echo in the small plane.

Of course, at that exact moment the airplane bumps with turbulence.

I manage to hold on to the flashlight without dropping it. I peek into the tank opening with one eye.

Depending on your outlook on life, the new tank is half-empty or half-full. When it comes to flying, I tend to be a half-full type of person. If I wasn't, I probably wouldn't have said yes to this trip. In other situations, I'm inclined toward half-empty. Jay has a tendency toward half-empty, which is the perfect attitude for a pilot. I'm much more comfortable in the company of a pilot who pessimistically thinks something could go wrong at any minute rather than one who is ignorantly happy.

Jay turns off the fuel transfer. I make a note in the log.

It's suddenly very quiet.

In mid-pencil stroke, I look up. This isn't good, I think.

The steady hum is missing. You know: the hum of the engine.

"Oh, shoot." I hear myself saying. "Oh, shoot" is likely the most common famous last words of numerous overly adventurous people through history.

My autonomic nervous system takes over my body, getting it ready for flight or fight. Up here at 19,000 feet I can hear nothing but my desperate heartbeat; it sounds like it's going to thump out of my chest at any moment. My brain's frontal lobes haven't caught up, though, and a strange, rational calm pervades my thinking. I wonder why my heart is reacting so. A second later, my brain catches up to the seriousness of the situation. I glance over at Jay and notice a glimmer of fear in his eyes. The engine didn't even sputter; it just stopped without warning.

Jay always says if the engine fails, the airplane will become a glider, and then we can ditch onto the ocean's surface. Our emergency kit contains a fully inflatable life raft, bottled water, dried food, sunscreen, tools, flares, matches, and a marine beacon. On board is one drysuit and one survival suit; these are waterproof suits we can don and survive in for a while in the cold 50 degree waters of the Atlantic. We practiced one afternoon on the beige carpet of my living room, wriggling and shoehorning these suits on in less than 60 seconds.

My mind flutters with thoughts of ditching. Will I be able to wriggle into my survival suit? Will the waves be calm? Will the winds be right? Will I be able to get the life raft out of the cabin before it inflates? Will there be sharks? A whole new universe of catastrophic challenges fills my thoughts. What will happen to us? Will we die? Is this our "strike three?"

The silence continues.

Jay swings into action. The engine is starving for fuel, perhaps from a loss of pressure from the tank when the lever was turned off. He flips on the fuel pump as a booster and waits for the Malibu to respond. A contingency plan could be to switch the fuel transfer back on, but too much switching can starve the engine further, killing it completely.

The silence continues.

Then, a faint noise. You have to strain to hear it. Another few seconds, and the engine's hum resumes. That beautiful steady drone is back. What Jay did worked. We're saved from death! Elation!

Perfectly poised, Jay says, "New procedure: We'll turn on the fuel pump from now on when we make a fuel transfer adjustment."

"Got it." I reply, businesslike.

We are both fast learners. We chatter about nothing, just to relieve the tension. Whew, that was too close a call. It takes a long time for my heart to slow down to normal.

Usually, Jay and I limit our conversation during flight. He calls it a sterile cockpit. I don't know if other pilots use this term or whether it comes from Jay's background as a surgeon. It might sound cold and unfriendly, but I know it helps improve our odds of success. In a high-risk, high-workload flight, it's logical to focus on the tasks at hand and avoid unnecessary distractions, such as extraneous chit-chat. I know some recreational pilots who are reckless enough to read novels in their cockpits, and I would never fly with them. I respect Jay's serious approach to flying.

Medicine and flying are Jay's two loves in life. After he sold his medical practice in Dallas, he started performing volunteer surgery in Central America, Asia, and Africa. An ophthalmologist, he specializes in cataract surgery. On this trip, he'll offer his expertise in two destinations, Kenya and Nepal. Twice I've gone with him to the Nepal hospital, but I haven't been to Africa with him, so I don't know what to expect there.

We have been monitoring both the short- and long-range radios and have managed to stay in touch with New York via the high frequency radio. A New York controller tells us to switch to another frequency to communicate with Santa

Maria, where we will be landing. The transmission is garbled and the radio cuts out.

"Did you understand that frequency?" Jay asks me.

I shake my head. "No way. It was too garbled." I still haven't gotten the knack of understanding the radio communications very well.

"Let's use the one on the chart," says Jay.

We dial in several numbers. Nothing works. I continue to experiment with different adjustments while Jay talks to an Air Portugal pilot on VHF, in hopes that he'll relay our position to Santa Maria Center. He does.

FAA regulations prohibit two pilots in separate airplanes to use the official stations to simply chit chat. They can transfer to another station and talk, or they can talk about official business, such as making a position report for another if one is unable.

I feel better knowing that someone knows where we are. The brand new high frequency radio must be broken; it's simply not transmitting despite our following all of the directions in the manual. After tinkering with it for hours, my frustration level is saturated, and I stop playing with it.

We've been in the air for over nine hours, an aquamarine sea the predominant scenery all day. Jay adjusts the radar to point downward. A red blob appears on the weather radar screen.

"Land ahoy, mates!" Jay shouts.

This time, a red blob is good news. It is Flores, the westernmost island of the Azores. The thought ignites our excitement. We strain our eyes to view a clump of clouds in the 11 o'clock position, nearly straight ahead. Below the clouds will likely be an island. All of my fears and concerns about ditching melt away, at least for now. I'm ready and anxious for this leg of the flight to end.

We reach the control center on VHF radio and request permission to descend. As the cloud formation passes on the left, Jay remarks, "There are rocks in those clouds." I peer out his window. Sure enough, Horta's towering black volcano breaks out of the center of the wispy clouds.

The next island is Santa Maria, our destination. Straight ahead is a forest green and russet chunk of terra firma, in the middle of the huge aqua ocean. In the bright afternoon sunlight, from thousands of feet above the island, we strain to look for a tiny, thin, long, gray patch that will be the runway. The island gets bigger as we lose altitude rapidly. As we perform the descent checklist, the airplane's flaps extend and the wheels lock into place.

Jay keys the radio's microphone. "Santa Maria Approach, November-Three-One-Three-Juliet-Mike, requesting visual approach."

"Three-Juliet-Mike, Santa Maria Approach, cleared to land," says the controller.

Jay locates the airstrip and noses the airplane down. Just to the right of the runway is a shallow turquoise bay, dotted with tiny foamy whitecaps and bordered by a strip of ivory sand. Jay pulls back the power, guides the plane directly over the runway, and flares the nose of the plane. The wheels touch down softly.

"Woohoo!" I shout.

As we taxi off the landing strip, my body slumps in relief. I'm thrilled that this flight is finally at its end. I'm overjoyed to be on the ground. A rainbow of colors assaults my heretofore all-blue day. The early summer's growth of emerald trees and shrubs, a peeling yellow building, a rusty red truck, and a variety of local people excite our visual senses at this Portuguese outpost. We've re-entered civilization after being in our own world all day.

Near the tiny airport terminal, a tall man waves at us to park near a twin engine airplane. We taxi from the runway to the parking apron. All the airplanes here are substantially bigger than the Malibu. I open the door and stumble down onto land. After nearly 11 hours in the cramped cockpit, it feels tremendous to straighten my legs and stretch without confinement. I take a deep, long breath of fresh air. I have a big smile on my face.

The tall man greets us in English, surprisingly, "Welcome to the Azores. I am Vic." The dark-haired man is dressed in business casual and has an air of confidence about him.

Jay and Vic strike up a conversation about the flight while I look for our Immigration and Customs papers. The airport officials ask us what the takeoff weight of the airplane is. That's how they figure the airport charges. Vic inquires about fuel for the airplane and hotel arrangements for Jay and me.

The Malibu needs fuel, enough to reach our next destination, but no more. We don't want to carry any more weight than what we have to in order to keep our costs as low as possible. We also don't want extra fuel because of the risk of explosion and fire if there's a crash.

"We need 250 liters," Jay says to Vic. Converting gallons to liters is one of hundreds of math conversions we'll do on the trip. Fahrenheit to Celsius, one time zone to another, feet to meters, dollars to *escudos*, English to Portuguese, FAA flight rules to ICAO (International Civil Aviation Organization) standards, English to European weather abbreviations, culture to culture. We can never relax in the air, but on the ground this trip is no cakewalk either.

While Jay supervises the fueling, I pull out two copies of the General Declaration forms we have prepared. These are standard forms that contain information about the airplane such as the type, model, serial number, and weight. It lists Jay's address, the plane's tail number, and that it's a private flight. It lists our flight routing, and the crew's names, birthdays, pilot license numbers, and passport numbers. It includes a list of passengers and cargo, of which we have neither, and a declaration of health. As pilot-in-command, Jay has to sign it.

The Portuguese Immigration officers are all business, but also somewhat easy-going. On an island like this, there is never much crime or scandal. They don't even look inside our passports; they simply give us two cards to be surrendered upon departure. In Customs, a lady searches our bags by hand. There is no fancy scanning equipment here. Vic leads us into the flight office where Jay completes a form and pays a landing fee. The officials are friendly, yet businesslike. Few words are spoken in all of these exchanges. We must have done the arrival paperwork correctly, I muse.

I wonder what time it is. A 4:00 a.m. departure plus a 10:44 flight plus a four-hour time change plus an hour of airport business. It's about 7:00 or 8:00 p.m., close enough to the end of the day for me.

Today, our advantages outnumbered our strikes, and the first leg has been successful. We mastered the weather, the terrain, and the equipment challenges we had. I'm proud of us. We're both elated, but too tired to show it much.

I ask about hotels.

"There is one in town and one near the airport," Vic mentions.

"Let's stay at the one closest to the airport," says Jay.

Vic drives us to the *Hotel do Aeroporto* only a few kilometers away and helps us check in. The desk clerk is friendly yet formal. He and Vic speak Portuguese. I look around at the lobby area. It's elegant and simple at the same time.

There is a dining room off to the left.

I ask how much the room will cost. No answer. I've seen people assume that if you own an airplane, you're just spewing with money but, of course, this isn't true. I want to know how much to expect before we commit (not that we have any bargaining power on this remote island). I ask again how much it will cost and am finally told 7,500 *escudos*. The exchange rate is 144 *escudos* to US $1. The room will cost us a little over US $50 per night, a very fair price.

Inside the hotel room, we smile at each other but are too tired to celebrate. We both collapse from exhaustion. We sleep for a long time, temporarily forgetting about our broken high frequency radio or how we're going to make it across the rest of the Atlantic.

7 July, 1995
Santa Maria, The Azores

"What kind of man would live where there is no daring? I don't believe in taking foolish chances, but nothing can be accomplished without taking any chance at all."

—Charles A. Lindbergh,
at a news conference after his trans-Atlantic flight

I love waking up in a strange new place. I skip out of bed and carefully tango through the hotel room's mismatched furniture to the bathroom. I study the shower's Portuguese plumbing and step in. The hot water that emerges feels wonderful on my skin. The soap smells like vanilla. In the soft water, I rinse longer. I'm so glad to have completed yesterday's flight.

Before we met, Jay had traveled to about 90 countries and I had visited 35 or so. A goal of mine is to explore 100 countries before I'm 50. I just turned 39. On this trip, I'll gain about 15 new ones. Together, we've sailed the Caribbean, toured Asia, and explored the United States and North America. We have shared dozens of hotel rooms, a few state-rooms on small yachts, and even a tent. We both consider traveling a fun adventure and a welcome break in the routine of home life. Most of the time, our style is to show up and hunt for what's available. Only occasionally do we book reservations ahead of time.

Today, Jay and I happily transform from pilots to tourists. I slip on blue jeans and a red t-shirt while Jay wears khaki trousers, a turquoise polo shirt, and his wide-brimmed floppy white sailor's hat. He's very conscious of the sun's effect on his skin and wears his hat everywhere outside. It's time to enjoy the destination without worrying about the next leg of the flight. I want to explore; I love exploring as much as Jay loves flying.

I talk to the desk clerk about how to get to town. "Do you speak English?" I ask.

"No." The tall dark man at reception emits a confidence, even a pride, about not speaking English.

"*Parlez-vous francais?*" I squeak.

"*Oui, madam.*"

"Ahh. *Tres bien, merci.*"

I ask my question in French, and suddenly the desk clerk is very helpful. It helps to have contingency options on the ground as well as in the air. He gives me a map (in French only - no English available), two free postcards, and a lot of good information on the island. The map is not very detailed, but I really like having one because often people's directions are incorrect. Plus, it's such a small place that I don't think we'll get lost. Usually I ask the hotel clerk where the bad parts of town are so I can avoid them for my personal safety, but I don't here. To do so would be an insult. This type of place has little or no crime. Everyone knows each other, and there's no easy escape from an island. It's too bad there are not more places like this on earth.

After breakfast at the hotel, Jay and I stroll, holding hands, into Vila do Porto, about three kilometers away. A wooden fence borders the dusty, unpaved road for miles. The island smells like a country farm. White houses with clay tile roofs and trees dot the countryside. It's peacefully quiet; my ears appreciate the lack of constant engine noise that was their reality for over ten hours yesterday. With an island, you might think tropical, but you would be wrong here. Santa Maria is far north of the equator, on the same latitude as the state of Virginia, and surrounded by the chilly, sometimes foreboding Atlantic. The fields, full of wild grasses, look like they could use some rain. But it won't rain today. Only a few clouds break up the solid blue sky. In the mild temperature and light breeze, the walk connects me with the earth and helps me momentarily forget about airplanes, flying, airports, and pilots.

The old town of Vila do Porto bears a classic European look. Pioneers, pirates, farmers, and traders fill the archipelago's history. In 1493, Christopher Columbus was returning from his historical discovery of the new world and stopped at this island. He was mistaken for a pirate by the locals, and his men were imprisoned until the situation could be straightened out a day or two later. Real pirates arrived throughout the fifteenth and sixteenth centuries. The farmers appeared later and were attracted by two plants, woad and archil, that were cultivated and used as ingredients in cloth dyes. The plants grew easily on the islands and made the local people very prosperous. In the middle of the nineteenth century, the crops lost their economic value when chemicals replaced them in the making of the dyes. The Santa Maria airport was built in 1944 by the United States, which used it as an Air Force base for many years. In the 1960s, when airplanes needed a fuel stop when crossing the Atlantic, the airport stayed busy serving the demand. The island of Santa Maria is tiny: only about 97 square kilometers. About 6,000 people live here today.

We spot 17th century stone fortress ruins and stride toward them. Wandering through Sao Bras Fort, we spy iron cannons aimed at the sea, still awaiting the next pirate ship's arrival. We silently read the historical plaques and contemplate what it would be like to live in those days. Jay recites what he remembers about the weapons and ammunition. He's happy and relaxed. The oceanside panorama here is breathtaking. Atlantic waves rhythmically crash against the hills and cliffs of the island. The air smells of sea salts and the fresh ocean breeze. I can feel the temperate breeze against my skin and wafting through my hair.

"I'm hungry. Let's go into town," says Jay. It's already mid-afternoon. We amble toward the city center and spot the one main street in Vila do Porto. We find a place to change money and stop for lunch in a nice restaurant.

Jay and I study the menu. "What are you going to get?"

I point to a dish with shrimp and rice that is listed on the menu instead of saying its name because the menu is in Portuguese and I can't pronounce the words. I know enough foreign languages to recognize, but not pronounce, rice and shrimp in several of them.

"That's what I was leaning towards," says Jay. We order the same thing about three-quarters of the time. We are unbelievably compatible when it comes to food. Our diets are almost identical: we are both vegetarians, except we also eat fish and shellfish. I prefer Pepsi, while Jay insists on Diet

Coke.

On the way back, I photograph a windmill, a remnant from the island's Dutch history dating back to the 15th century when small groups of Flemish people settled on the islands. We find a wonderful road that leads us to a hill that overlooks the town. We take advantage of this Kodak moment.

"Can we stop at the airport?" Jay asks.

But it's not really a question. Jay has now gone several hours without seeing his plane, so he must be having withdrawal symptoms. Airports are magnetic to Jay; he can't go past one without stopping in. I tag along, not too excited about this particular tourist stop, but also knowing in the back of my mind that Jay's enthusiasm is a good thing.

An employee at the Santa Maria airport says we can't depart with a broken high frequency radio. If we can't fix it on the island, we have to wait to leave in tandem with another aircraft going to Faro, Portugal, our next destination, that can relay our flight positions. Normally, it would be nice to be stranded on a beautiful European island. But we can't give ourselves permission to relax; it's just too early in the trip for that.

At the hotel, Jay faxes an urgent note on hotel stationery to Northeast Air, the maintenance company that installed the plane's extra gas tank and high frequency radio. He writes them about the broken radio, informing them of our predicament, and includes comments about the air bubble we experienced with the auxiliary gas tank when the engine temporarily stopped yesterday. We contemplate renting a car, but spend time writing postcards instead. The day dashes by. The island doesn't offer any nightlife, and that's fine with Jay and me. We sit down to a quiet dinner at the hotel restaurant, then retire early to the room. Our plan is to spend two to three more days here before heading for the European mainland.

In the morning, Jay rises early to run 10 kilometers for exercise. I sit in bed, waking gradually and writing in my diary.

Suddenly Jay bursts back into the room much earlier than it takes to run 10K. "A Concorde has landed!" he shouts excitedly. He's out of breath. "I have to get a picture of the Malibu and the Concorde together!" He grabs his camera and runs back out of the room. For you and me, that's better than getting your picture made with Madonna.

Late morning, there is no fax response yet from Northeast Air. Jay returns and changes out of his running clothes. He rinses them and hangs them to dry on anything he can find around the hotel room. I'm lucky Jay does his own laundry and doesn't expect me to do that kind of chore for him. We walk toward town and, elatedly, he recounts his visit with the Concorde. His passion for airplanes is overflowing. I can see the scrapbook value of the picture for Jay, and I smile at him. Jay's enthusiasm about flying is part of what will keep us alive.

We stop at the airport on our walk to town. We need to find a plane going to Faro. The Air France Concorde departed from Paris; its target is Martinique in the Caribbean. (Not that we could keep up with it anyway.) Another airplane is leaving for the Canary Islands. No one is traveling to Faro. We're stuck. At the airport, Jay and Vic deliberate on our predicament.

After much discussion, Vic says, "Just file and go." He must sense Jay's anxiety about being stuck here. The airport employee on today's shift is unacquainted with our radio problem, and he echoes Vic. "Just file and go." The tower staff is unaware as well. So we shift into high gear. We file our flight plan to Faro and make preparations to leave as fast as we can before someone changes his mind. This is earlier than we planned, but sometimes you have to act on an opportunity when it arises. Jay dispatches me to the hotel to pack and check out while he remains at the airport readying the plane. We quickly morph from tourists back into an air crew team with an important mission to accomplish.

Our clothes and toiletries are scattered all over the hotel room. Jay's running shorts are still wet from that morning's run. I throw our things haphazardly into each of our suitcases and walk down to the hotel reception desk to check out.

"*L'addition, s'il vous plait*," I ask the hotel clerk, requesting the bill.

"*Oui, Madame.*" The hotel clerk continues slowly in French, explaining to me very politely that a hotel bill was "*une note*" or even "*un facture*," and not what I called it, which is how you ask a waiter for the check at a restaurant. At least he knew what I meant.

"*Voila*," I exclaim, trying to act very French. "*Merci pour une lecon de francais.*"

I hand the desk clerk my credit card, and we complete our exchange.

At the airport, I fill out the paperwork for Immigration and Customs, using full sheets of carbon paper for the first time in years while Jay preps the plane and obtains a weather briefing. Isolated thunderstorms surround Faro, but clear skies are reported en route.

During their conversation, Jay and Vic hit it off when Vic discovers Jay is a "doctor of mercy," meaning Jay volunteers his medical services in countries less economically advantaged than the United States. Vic turns out to be a colorful character himself. Besides having the best English of anyone we talked to on this island, he is retired from being Santa

Maria's airport manager and once helped arrange housing for NASA workers during a large weather project. Jay gives him two of his prized Diet Cokes and a Fortune magazine. Guy bonding, I guess.

Finally inside the plane we taxi to the runway in preparation for takeoff. I mentally prepare myself for another long over-water flight. I punch in the squawk code and start entering the waypoints into the GPS.

Suddenly the GPS database flickers, and its display turns dark. "What happened? I can't punch in the waypoints for the flight," I tell Jay.

"The GPS is dead." Jay is dismayed, but only temporarily. He transforms an event like this into a challenge to be overcome. He believes his training will support him in many scenarios. All he has to do to get through any difficulty is remember his training. I think this is how he gets through any fears that might come up as well.

"Well, it would be difficult to miss an entire continent." Jay muses.

I laugh.

"Let's focus on the takeoff," he says, all business. Stopping now is not a good option. The airport employees could ground us for several days.

"Roger that," I reply. We continue as if nothing has gone wrong.

Jay tunes in the Santa Maria Island VOR (Very high frequency Omnidirectional Radio) frequency on the radio so that we can have ground signal navigation. Over the Atlantic, where there won't be any VORs, we'll be navigating by dead reckoning.

At 1:00 p.m. local time on the third day of the Atlantic portion of our adventure, it's "wheels up" for the Malibu. The sun is high in the sky with no clouds in sight. I wonder what we've done to deserve two major equipment problems this early in the trip. How will the trip evolve if this rash of problems continues?

In flying, it's sensible to duplicate as much equipment as you possibly can because, at some point, you'll likely need it. Most of the main instruments display on both the pilot's side and the copilot's side in the cockpit. Redundant speed indicators, attitude indicators, turn displays, altimeters, rate of climb indicators, and compasses fill the instrument panel. Two yokes and two sets of rudder pedals offer redundant control tools. If one piece of equipment goes out, you can always rely on the backup system. This redundancy greatly reduces the risks of flying and increases any pilot's chances for survival. If you think about it, nature follows the same redundancy rule. Humans have two arms, two lungs, two ears, et cetera.

A pilot can navigate in a multitude of ways. By means of GPS, a pilot selects the waypoints for the flight, and the GPS displays the heading that is to be flown. Using VOR and DME (Distance Measuring Equipment), an airman can receive land-based radio signals from which he can determine the course, speed, and distance to fly. VOR and DME operate within 200 nautical miles of land or an aircraft carrier, but not over the open sea. ADF (Automatic Direction Finder) functions between a beacon on the ground that gives signals and antennae on the airplane that receives the signals. It produces a bearing with which to compute the airplane's direction. NDB (Non-Directional Beacon) works like a station broadcast, covering about a thousand-mile range. A directional gyro in the instrument panel, slaved to a magnetic fluxgate compass in the airplane's wing, operates in most conditions. If all else fails, a good old-fashioned magnetic compass serves as the final backup tool.

In Portland, we had to adjust the magnetic compass in a procedure called "swinging the compass." Whenever you add additional metal to a plane, like the auxiliary fuel tank, the compass needs to be reset. An engineer taxis the plane and points it in each of the four directions - north, east, south, and west - and corrects the compass readings for each direction.

After takeoff, I reach in the flight bag, grab the handheld GPS that we brought as a backup to the plane's built-in GPS, and compute the bearing. The air traffic controller instructs us to fly south until we reach an altitude of 3,500 feet, then we can turn left toward Europe. The battery on the GPS is already low, so I leave my seat and crawl in the back to track down the battery pack.

I can't spot it.

There's another *POP!!* It's just the gas tank top blowing its lid again as the cabin becomes pressurized.

I recap the gas tank and then hunt for the battery pack to the Garmin GPS receiver. I can't find it. Jay finally deduces the problem. He brought the wrong accessory for the handheld GPS.

So let's take inventory. No high frequency radio, no main GPS, no handheld GPS. Our usual LORAN database is worthless because it contains only North American waypoints. In Virginia, we lost a gyro - a turn indicator/coordinator - on the copilot's (my) side. We resort to navigating by VOR, until the signal becomes too weak to read. We'll be traveling imprecisely for most of the 800 nautical miles in this voyage. It's fearful to think we will be over the vast ocean with no one else knowing exactly where we are. If something goes wrong, it will be harder for a rescue crew to find our location.

A turquoise sea swirls beneath us. The Atlantic has a reputation for being a terrifying place to sail. I gape downward to try to glimpse any whitecaps, but we're too high to spot them. The sound of the engine is steady, and the smell of gasoline is constantly present.

We're tracking away from the Santa Maria VOR signal. The plane is drinking fuel from the auxiliary tank, which has to be watched closely. We reach our first checkpoint, EKROL. Jay reports our position before we lose Santa Maria on VHF radio. We're still climbing. Observing the gauges, I notice the cylinder head needle reads near redline. That means the engine is close to overheating. In my mind, I silently curse this instrument and the stress I feel from it on every flight.

We overhear another pilot reporting his plane's position at BRAVO waypoint.

"They must be flying from Lajes Air Force Base," comments Jay.

Once we lose the Santa Maria VOR signal, we'll need a pilot that's flying nearby to relay our position to the air traffic controllers. This will compensate for us not having a working high frequency radio. Without the HF radio, we don't have long-distance, over-water communication. But with our VHF radio, we can communicate with nearby airplanes, whose pilots can then radio the faraway centers for us. When the pilot reports, "MAKIN next," Jay knows he has a possibility for a relay. MAKIN is our next waypoint too.

After a while, Jay asks for the favor. "Otis Seven-One, this is November-Three-One-Three-Juliet-Mike requesting a relay."

There is a pause.

"Three-Juliet-Mike, Otis Seven-One, go ahead." It's a male voice. American. A comforting thought.

Pilots and air traffic controllers all over the world must conduct international air traffic radio communications in

English, the official language of aviation. Chaos would reign if aviators had to learn and use 20 different languages. It's difficult enough to comprehend static-filled radio transmissions, non-standard commands, stepped-on broadcasts, and regional accents.

"Otis-Seven-One, November-Three-One-Three-Juliet-Mike checked MAKIN at 1530, Flight Level One-Niner-Zero, estimating 38 North 20 West at 1620, 38 North 16 West next," reports Jay. He also explains to the pilot that we have just begun to navigate by dead reckoning.

"Juliet-Mike, copy that. Will relay."

Jay and the pilot communicate some more. Otis Seven-One identifies itself as US Marine Corps flying a hercky-bird (short for Hercules), or a C-130 transport plane, about 100 miles behind us. Well, that's a nice break in our luck. I'm comfortable traversing the Atlantic with US Marines flying in our airspace. I can dig that any day. Jay labels him our guardian angel for this trip. Bursting with pride, Jay briefly shares our round-the-world goals with the Marine.

It's a good thing George still works. George is the pet name for the autopilot. It mostly helps to free a pilot's hands from the yoke. Slaved to the navigation system, speed and altitude gauges, it keeps the plane on course, speed, and altitude. When the workload becomes heavy, George helps us out a lot. It still has to be monitored, of course, but it's nice to be able to periodically free your hands for other tasks, such as finding the next chart, making a radio call, writing down a frequency, or updating the fuel log.

After an hour of flying, Otis Seven-One's aviator volunteers to identify our position using his own plane's onboard radar system. We squawk code 1300 on our radar transponder, and the marine locates a spot on his radar at 38 North, 18 West. Their faster speed has overtaken us, however, and shortly we fall out of range. Otis Seven-One will reach the mainland much sooner than we will.

Now that our guardian angel is gone, it would be most inopportune for an emergency to happen. We don't have direct contact with the mainland; we won't know exactly where we are for a while. We could have trouble raising anyone on the radio. We just have to hope our luck will hold up a little while longer.

A few clouds appear in the sky. Some are light and wispy, almost transparent. Others are round and full. The sun catches the edges of one, leaving a bright gold outline that marvels the senses. To witness the clouds from above instead of below is one of the miracles of flight. Fear and beauty sometimes go together.

We reach our next checkpoint, and it's time for a position report. With Otis Seven-One no longer around, there are no aircraft in range that can relay our position. Jay tunes the VHF into Lisbon Center, on the wild chance that it will work. We're thrilled when it does. He makes the report. Now that we have a VHF frequency, our radio challenges are over until we reach the Mediterranean Sea. It's a huge relief to know we don't have to dead reckon any more and that someone actually knows where we are. Plus, it means that there is an end to this flight; we'll reach the mainland in an hour or two.

After three and a half hours of sitting, I feel restless. It would be nice to be able to get up and walk around. Most of all, I need to go to the bathroom. There is no restroom on board. No separate ladies' room. No stall with a nice private partition. Nothing to sit on, nothing that flushes. Jay has gone one or two times already, right there in his seat, using "his" toilet, a relief tube.

This is the type of gender inequity that gives me pause. Men can simply remain seated in the cockpit without unbuckling their seat belts. They can whip out the relief tube, do their thing, and *voila*, they're finished. I know women pilots flying alone who have had to land before they reach their destination. Considering the fuel and wear and tear on the airplane, that's a pretty expensive potty break. Over the oceans, we don't even have that choice.

In this case, I designed a gender-specific process worthy, I believe, of all female aviators before and after me. When nature calls, I rise, slink to the back without the benefit of a private bathroom stall, in full view of the heavens *and* Jay (who is gentleman enough not to look), and commune with my trusty mayonnaise jar. Then I pour the contents of the mayonnaise jar down the relief tube and chase it with a little sodium bicarbonate in hopes of neutralizing any scent.

For women who fly solo, long-distance flying poses a special dilemma. To get out of your seat is a safety issue and something to be avoided. Amelia Earhart did not have this problem solved either; a Newark airplane mechanic mentioned to an aviation designer that after one of her long-distance flights, the inside of her plane smelled of urine. Normally, Amelia was impeccably clean and tidy, so this challenge must have been upsetting for her. Short of wearing adult diapers, I'm not sure what modern aviatrixes do to conquer this problem.

When I return to my seat, Jay is munching on a package of Doritos and slurping a Diet Coke. I crinkle my nose at the smell of Doritos; I can't stand their aroma. The airplane food "served" aboard the Malibu leaves something to be desired. During a flight, I do not eat or drink much; I prefer to wait until after we've landed and I have access to "real" restrooms as often as I want.

Cumulus clouds envelop Faro as we approach the city whose name means "lighthouse." Taking my turn to fly, I intercept the controls from George and fly the descent. My hands clutch the yoke, and I point the airplane's nose down. I grip harder, trim the ailerons, and steady the yoke. The Malibu races to the ground. I pull the power back a little. I glance out at each wing to make sure the plane is level. To keep the wings perfectly even, I make tiny adjustments. At my skill level, I have to concentrate hard. Flying doesn't come naturally for me, but when I can control the airplane, I feel a sense of accomplishment.

The coastline peeks out occasionally from behind the clouds and haze. A jagged white line of waves crashes against the hilly brown continent. Slowly, the land grows larger and larger. I dodge more clouds as we reach the lower altitudes. Soon, I can no longer avoid the clouds, so Jay must take over. Raindrops gently stroke the plane.

We're in touch with the air traffic controller, who asks us in his Portuguese accent to make a circle for spacing. This happens when there are too many planes approaching the runway at the same time. I watch Jay do a perfect 360 degree turn; these maneuvers are terrific practice to keep flying skills in shape. For a beginner like me, the trick is to focus on maintaining a consistent altitude at the same time one is performing a controlled turn, watching the power, and reacting to the winds. *Whew!* I'm dizzy just thinking about it.

We land in light rain and taxi off the runway. Both of us are pretty excited about making it across the Atlantic. I can feel butterflies - the good kind - in my chest. Jay is smiling. I'm ready to do a cheer. A small white truck with a large "Follow Me" sign leads the way to parking and waits for us. We park near a dozen other small aircraft. Jay shuts down the plane and tries to extract the broken GPS in case we can find a repair shop. He can't get it out. He needs a 3/32 Allen wrench, a size that's not in the standard American set. He makes a note and leaves it for now.

I exit the plane and stop to take a deep fresh breath. Even though it's raining, the air is cleaner than the stuffy air in the cabin that is full of avgas fumes. It's a relief to my body to inhale the fresh air. The temperature is mild, in the sixties, and feels pleasant. The engine sounds of cars, planes, and trucks fill my ears.

Outside the plane, Jay stoops and kisses the ground. I smile and take the requisite photo. We have traversed one ocean. It's a moment for celebration. We do a little dance in the rain, like when a football player intercepts the ball and makes an unexpected touchdown. It will be quite a while before we face the challenge of ocean flying again. The driver in the follow-me car watches all of this, smiling. He waits patiently as we unload our bags, tie down the plane, and block the wheels with chocks.

The airport is a nice-sized one for a small European town. It's quite a drive from parking to the airport buildings. The driver of the follow-me truck speaks only Portuguese, so we smile and don't say much. We stow our already damp bags in the follow-me truck and hop in for a ride to the airport office to complete a landing form. Here, the officials do speak English. Mostly they tell us what paperwork we need and how much we owe them. Then it's on to Passport Control where we pass through the crew line, just like a commercial airline crew. A worker at the tourist office helps us reserve a hotel room in the city center, right across from the train station. We hail a taxi. Jay hates taking taxis; it's one of his quirks. But this time, it's the best choice of transportation, and the hotel is only five minutes away.

Hotel Faro is located off of a wonderful square, bustling with pigeons, pedestrians, tourists, and street vendors. The ocean is only a few blocks away. It's the perfect location for a hotel, one that generates its own vibrant energy and feels like the center of everything. The old city, a tourist destination, is nearby. So are the bus station and a marina. I am thrilled with this hotel. What a great choice! I love staying in the center of everything, where it's so close to walk to so many sights. In the lobby, we shake off the rain as well as we can and check in at the desk.

The second-story room is spacious by European standards and well-decorated. It's air-conditioned, but we open the balcony door instead and let the fresh air in. On the private patio outside our room, Jay can watch the jets land while sitting in the sunshine. On the TV station in the hotel room, I catch a glimpse of home with Americans Karen McGinnis and Linden Soles on CNN. The news report broadcasts an update of the O. J. Simpson trial. Well, it's nice to be reminded of back home, but I think I've had all I need. I turn off the TV and enjoy Portugal instead.

Jay purchases a phone card and calls his mom and dad, friends in Monroe, Louisiana, and just about everyone he knows. "We crossed the ocean. We made it!" he exclaims to everyone.

I call my mom and dad to share the milestone.

"Hi, Mom. We're in Portugal," I say excitedly.

"Hi, Sandi. Good for you. I'm glad you're safe," Mom replies.

I can visualize Mom's fair skin, coifed red hair, and Dutch blue eyes. At 68 years, her frame has shrunk a bit from her 5'6" height. Mom's always struggled with her weight, calling herself big-boned. What I remember about her the most is her beautiful smile.

"How is everyone?" I ask.

"Everyone's fine here. Your cat is fine too," Mom answers.

Six-year-old Molly, a tortoiseshell female, lives with me in Dallas. When I travel, my mom and dad are gracious enough to keep her, so I don't have to place her in a boarding house for pets.

"I love you and I'll call you next week," I say, hanging up the receiver. I'm lucky to have the parents I do. Filled with beauty and generosity, my mom has a lot of love for the world. My dad is a wise, steady, and supporting force in my life. Both are huge supporters of me going on this journey.

After the phone calls, the rain stops and the sun peeks out. Hungry, we feast at a nearby Chinese restaurant. I love using chopsticks and am quite proficient at it. When we finish, the waitress gives me a nice pair of chopsticks as a souvenir. It is nearly midnight when we reach the hotel, and the sun has just barely set. It feels really great to be in Europe with Jay and the Malibu. I feel very lucky to be here.

Our preparation for this part of the journey has paid off. The ultimate measure of success in flying is that of being alive and healthy, and we have accomplished that much. We have many more legs to fly, however, before we cross the finish line back in Dallas. I don't know what challenges await us, but I know there will be many.

9 July, 1995
Faro, Portugal

"Life is an irresistible activity, a never-hesitating, struggling, and triumphant growth."

—*Henri Bergson*

*F*rom Faro, we rest from flying for a few days and complete a whirlwind tour of four countries: Portugal, Spain, Gibraltar, and Morocco. Jay is adamant about traveling all the way through Portugal and Spain to see Gibraltar, even though I have been there before and am sure I'll be bored. But we also ferry across the Mediterranean to Tanger, Morocco, which is new to me. I've always wanted to see the famed Kasbah. The next couple of days will be a chance for me to see both old and new sights.

Each of these destinations offers something fantastic and unique to the traveling explorer. Traveling affords us a fascinating study of people, places, and relationships. In Faro, we spend a day walking around and touring the city. In the Manuel Bivar Gardens, kids play with pigeons, and Jay treats himself to an ice cream. Walking through an archway, Arco da Vila, we enter the old city with its cobblestone streets and buildings dating from the 16th through the 18th centuries. In the square, Largo da Se, we see a statue of Bishop Francisco Gomes, who helped rebuild the city after a 1755 earthquake. I love the picturesque homes with colorful flowers perched outside the second story windows. A square wouldn't be complete without a cathedral, and some say this one is built atop a Moorish mosque from the 13th century. The streets are narrow and contain only a few shops, nicely limiting the commercialism of the place. We wander through the streets near the hotel. Being Sunday, most of the shops are closed. At a nearby sidewalk café, we eat pizza and salad for dinner in the sunshine. The scene is semi-romantic, even for Jay and me, neither of who is very demonstrative in public. In the evening, back in the hotel room, we study all of the tourist brochures and bus schedules that we acquired today and make a game plan for tomorrow's adventure.

In the morning we try to rent a car, but no one wants us to take it across the border to Spain. So we leave some bags at Hotel Faro and catch a train to Via Real de San Antonio. From the train, we transfer to a ferry. From the ferry, we walk across this small town peppered with quaint cafes and young, energetic Europeans to where the bus leaves for Huelvas. The bus driver is grouchy and speaks no English. Maybe it's because of that really bad bus accident that just happened in France, or maybe he's just a grouch. We get off at Sevilla so we can get another bus to Algeciras. But first we have to go across town, on the C-3 bus to the other bus station. Confused? So are we. We don't see any other tourists. We must be off the beaten tourist track for sure.

Jay is antsy. "Are you sure this is the best way to get to Gibraltar?"

"The Malibu would have been the best way to get to Gibraltar," I quip. We might just be better at air transportation than we are at ground transportation.

Jay scowls at the idea of the extra expense of fuel and landing fees. "We should have just rented a car and driven across the border anyway," he decides. Jay is more inclined to bend a rule and take full responsibility for whatever happens. Once in St. Martin, he took a yacht and me all the way to Barbados without permission. Nothing happened, but if it had, Jay would have covered it. I tend to be more respectful of rules. I'm sure it's because I'm a CPA, and you know what happens to companies and economies if we bend the rules. It's not a good thing.

But it's too late now for regrets and contingency plans. In Sevilla, the Spanish locals are helpful and friendly, even during their rush hour, which is when we catch them. Sevilla is a big city, replete with auto exhaust, traffic horns, motorcycle engines, and tire screeches. Before we can get on the bus to Algeciras, we need to buy tickets but we don't have enough *pesetas*. Jay leaves me holding the bags - literally - and runs to find someone on the street to change money with. I panic; he only has a couple of minutes before the last bus leaves. He runs back, out of breath, and we each buy a ticket and settle onto the bus. This bus driver - our third today - plays his favorite Spanish radio station the whole way to Algeciras.

Spain's countryside reminds me very much of West Texas. Herds of cattle, sheep, and goats populate the ranches, and crops fill the farm's fields here. The only differences are the occasional castle, church, or ruin that pepper the Spanish scenery. For just a moment I think I really am in Texas until I see a castle and am jolted back into the non-routine of the current journey.

One train, one ferry, and three busses later, we arrive in Algeciras. It's nearly midnight and we crash at Hotel Octavio, a very American-like hotel with a mini-bar and a shower head that is fixed in the wall. In the morning, we see Tanger, Morocco via a tour.

The Africa Tours bus takes us to the tour headquarters and later the ferry terminal via a 25-kilometer drive to Tarifa, a town we passed last night. We ride a ferry across the Mediterranean to Morocco. The ferry's engine is loud and fast, although to me it seems like a slow crossing. Many other nationalities are present on the ferry: Germans, French, Japanese, Chinese, and even a few Americans. It's fun to hear five different languages at once and try to figure out what each one is. Jay and I climb on the top level of the ferry so we can get the best view of the Mediterranean crossing. The wind hits us as we walk on deck, and we both grab our hats before they disappear overboard. My face feels the sea spray and my hair blows all over in the stiff ocean breeze, which feels good, but cool. We strain our eyes to see the African coastline and the individual cities on this southerly and westerly route. The boat sways and creaks as it speeds through the water, and I keep my feet wide apart and my knees bent to maintain my balance. On the boat we pass through Immigration and Customs. The temperature warms as we approach noon and also as we move farther south.

Off the boat, we join our guide, Akmen, and board an air-conditioned tourist bus along with about 40 other tourists. Akmen wears a black-and-white vertically striped robe with wide sleeves and a white head-covering. He's a small, elderly, lanky man who strikes me as brilliant. He speaks six languages and gives the tour in four: English, Spanish, Italian, and German.

The bus driver takes us through town, where we view many churches and religious temples of all kinds. Muslims, Catholics, and other religions live here together peacefully, Akmen emphasizes, as if it's a message to the world. The Muslims pray five times a day. Almost all the buildings are white, giving the cityscape a bright glow and a holy look. We reach the edge of the famed Kasbah, and I feel a tingle of excitement as if I'm a little kid again.

As soon as we disembark the bus, vendors accost us, selling leather, fezzes, brass items, wallets, bracelets, handicrafts, and more. Each salesperson jams the goods in our faces until we say, "No." Then they go to the next person and do the same thing.

The guide leads us through the labyrinth streets and into shops where many of the tourists on our bus buy souvenirs. One purchases a bird cage, another chooses a wallet, and still another acquires an entire Moroccan outfit: robe and fez. After the shops, we dutifully follow the group to a postcard stand and later a snake show. Well, what it actually is is people draping this snake over their friends' shoulders and snapping a picture. Jay and I pass on the shops and the snakes. For one thing, we still have to watch our weight or at least the airplane does. Anything we buy would have to be shipped home immediately. Plus, we're both just not that materialistic, preferring to spend our money on experiences instead of things.

"Did you notice that the only people wearing fezzes are the tourists and the fez vendors?" Jay observes.

I laugh. "You're right!"

The streets are really a maze; I don't know how anyone finds their way around. They are narrow and unmarked and wind around and around in a confusing puzzle. I stay close to the group; a bit fearful of getting left behind in this labyrinth. Local ladies wear veils or handkerchiefs over their faces. There are clothing shops selling robes and veils, markets selling local vegetables and fruits, shops offering brass objects of every kind, carpet shops selling oriental rugs, and jewelry stores selling trinkets. The buildings stand on average three stories tall and look like boxes stacked carelessly on top of one another. The shops are packed tightly next to each other, and there isn't much room for tourists, vendors, merchandise, and guides in such a tiny place. We are led quite a ways through these fascinating streets. It's a beautiful, hot day, but in these streets, it's much cooler.

Soon, we have lunch. Forty of us pile onto a bench around a U-shaped table in a private room and are served vegetable soup, shish kabobs, couscous with carrots and cabbage, and a dry cookie. We sit next to a family who lives in Garland, a Dallas suburb. Jay strikes up a conversation with the man of the house. The woman is originally from Brazil and shares her handi-wipes with everyone. The Japanese lady takes her handi-wipe and cleans her glass, silverware, and bowl. The next thing you know, everyone at the table is doing the same thing. I just chuckle under my breath. I really enjoy human nature at its most raw moments. It can be quite telling.

Jay and I, being vegetarian, pass on the shish kabobs when they come around but enjoy the remainder of the meal very much. We whisper to each other things about what we noticed today, almost gossiping like soap opera watchers. Four musicians serenade us, and we all get so caught up in meeting new friends and talking over the noise that we forget to listen to the music. A belly dancer, who is not thin like a model but not obese either, comes out during dessert. Her outfit shimmers with gold satin and sequins as she shimmies to the music. Everyone except Jay enjoys the dancer. Jay feels hot and opens the shutter behind him to catch some breeze. No such luck. The last thing that's served is some hot tea.

After a long winding walk, our tourist group files back on the bus and is taken for a countryside drive. Palm trees line the roadsides. We are shown big fancy houses on a street named California, not an unusual sight for the United States, but maybe an unusual sight for Europeans.

"Wonder why that's on the tour," I comment to Jay, not expecting an answer. Some remote countries really don't know how to handle tourists or know what they like. But Morocco would certainly not be in that category, would it?

We stop at a rest stop, and everyone files out of the bus. Here we can buy drinks, ride a camel for 100 *pesetas*, buy postcards, and stretch our legs. It's a bit dusty and hot at this stop. I buy five postcards and take pictures of the camel, which happens to have a baby with it. It doesn't look too friendly; it's just being a protective mom, I'm sure. The baby is cute and fun to watch. The last stop is a Kodak moment on a hazy lookout. I'll have to admit I don't take many pictures of Morocco's sights; instead I have too much fun taking pictures of tourists falling for tourist traps.

The bus takes us back to the ferry terminal and we file onto the catamaran once again. The line to board the boat is long. We have to go through Immigration and Customs, but this time it's complicated. We have to copy a number from the passport stamp onto the exit card, which is way too hard for most tourists. Although we're promised a 6:30 p.m. arrival time, we don't reach the hotel until 9:00 p.m.

"I'm starving. Think we can find something open this late?" I ask.

"Me too. No problem, this is Europe. Everything is open late." Jay replies.

Before we even sit down in the hotel room, we go straight
back out to find dinner. Walking down the street on the way
to the marina, I feel a touch of vertigo from all the busses and
ferries we've taken the last few days. Vertigo is mostly a fun,
lightheaded feeling for me, though. I feel like I've had a
drink without the alcohol. Once, about a decade ago, I spent
three weeks on a small yacht with four other people, and
when I returned to work, I remember walking in a zigzag
down a long corridor, thinking the walls were moving.

For our late dinner, we find just the place with a modest
menu and a table outdoors. We both enjoy soup, bread, and
wine, and Jay devours fish while I consume an omelet. We
enjoy the starlit skies, cool evening temperature, and fresh
air. Today was a productive day with lots of interesting
sights, and we talk about what we experienced. Tomorrow
we tackle Gibraltar.

In the morning, we head straight for the bus station and
take the 8:30 bus to LaLinea, which is right across the border
from Gibraltar. It's a warm sunny day. Jay dresses in khaki
shorts and a maroon polo shirt. I wear my green short shorts
and a white t-shirt top with thin green stripes and a green
collar. I wear a white visor and Jay wears his floppy white
hat. In my red backpack are my camera, some sunscreen,
bug repellent, a guide book, and my purse. After fifty minutes on the bus, we depart and head for the border, a short
quarter-mile walk. Showing our passports, we cross into
Gibraltar and head for the rock.

Most of Gibraltar is this one huge rock. There is a winding switchback you can walk up to reach the top, but we
cheat and take the tram up. Then we leisurely walk down,
seeing the sights on the way. St. Michael's Cave takes only a
few minutes to explore. Inside the cave is a lake and multi-
tudes of stalagmites and stalactites to see. The Moorish

Castle overlooks the Strait of Gibraltar, keeping guard over the place. Made of stones, the tall structure looks very old and in a bit of disrepair.

On the way down, we can't miss the famous Gibraltar apes. These inquisitive creatures are the size of a four-year-old child and will come right up to you. As I am changing film on my camera, an ape nearly takes my roll of film.

"Hey!" I scold, as if the ape can understand me.

Jay watches the whole scene and is laughing under his breath. I just don't have enough hands to change the film, hold the old roll, hold the camera, and manage my backpack. I grab at the roll of film, dangerously close to the ape.

The ape bites me. I let out a yelp. My hand shows teeth marks, but the ape doesn't break the skin. The ape drops the roll and the drama is over. I let out a sigh of relief.

On Main Street, we find the Maharaja Indian restaurant and have a mid-day meal.

Before we leave Gibraltar, Jay goes on a treasure hunt for the 3/32 Allen wrench he needs to get the GPS out. This may be the only place where we can find the right size. After much searching, Jay finds a tiny hardware shop on the back streets of Gibraltar and greets a British man wearing thick glasses. The man locates the size of Allen "key" that we need.

We catch the 3:15 p.m. bus to Seville, stopping at Algeciras to get our bags from Hotel Octavio. While paying the bill at the hotel, it seems someone helped themselves to the vodka in our mini-bar. Jay signs a paper that it wasn't him, and we are on our way back to Portugal.

In Seville, we spend the night at Hotel Monte Carlo and eat fish sandwiches at a McDonald's just around the corner. Jay and I stop at McDonald's when we're traveling in foreign lands and just need something familiar to latch onto. From

Thailand to France, McDonald's food is eerily consistent and a taste we can count on.

We take the first morning bus to Faro and make it back a little after noon.

"Let's go to the beach." says Jay.

"I really don't feel like a beach, right now. I need to wash clothes and run errands this afternoon," I say gently. Jay is dismayed and goes to the beach alone.

I wander around in the local shops, buying things that I need, such as cereal for mornings when breakfast doesn't come with the room and envelopes to mail souvenirs back to Texas. I leisurely catch up writing in my diary, and I wash clothes in a nearby washateria. Frequently, I will wash a few pieces in the hotel sink, but when I have a lot, it makes sense to find a washing machine and dryer. Plus, I find it fun to use foreign coins and interpret the machine directions in the foreign languages. It feels like a little victory of daily life when I can get clean clothes all by myself in such a strange setting.

Sometimes I need a day off from the sightseeing. That might sound spoiled, but anything to excess can become weary. I watch the O. J. Simpson trial on TV and hear the lawyers argue about racism. That world seems planets away from where we are and what we have been doing since we started this journey two weeks ago. When Jay returns from the beach, we find a Chinese restaurant for dinner.

In the morning, we head for the Faro airport. At Information, we find out how to proceed through all of the airport checkpoints. A man leads us through Ticket Control, X-ray, and to General Aviation. In the weather office, we receive a "met," a meteorological forecast. Next, we file the fight plan in the Planning Office. The flight plan is a standardized form that looks the same in most countries except for the language. This one is in Portuguese and English. Jay enters the aircraft tail number and type of plane. The Malibu is a PA-46. He writes in the speed, flight level, route, destination airport code, estimated time en route, first and second alternate airport codes, his address, and the emergency information. This includes how many hours of fuel are on board, how many people are on board, and what type of survival equipment, emergency radios, and rafts we have on board. We have to do this for every flight.

In the planning office, we also receive the NOTAMs (Notice to Airmen) which are notifications of things like airport construction, restricted airways, and other conditions that may not show on the printed charts we have of the area. In the airport office, we pay service and parking fees based on the gross weight of the airplane. A truck transports us from the airport offices to where the plane is parked. We need gasoline, so a fuel truck meets us to fill the plane. After all that, we can climb in and get ready to depart. Today it's a short ride to Palma de Mallorca, a beautiful Spanish Mediterranean island.

Upon departure, the plane is heavy with fuel. We fly at an altitude of 13,000 feet over Spain and then above the azure sea, landing on the island of Palma. The flight is a comfortable three hours with good weather, friendly governments, and easy terrain. A follow-me truck greets us, just like in Portugal. He shows us to the military apron at first. Jay radios clarification, and then we are shown to General Aviation. It was probably our November tail number that misled the follow-me driver into thinking we were military. Each airplane is uniquely identified with a tail number. Ours is N313JM. The N or November means we are US-based. March 13th happens to be Jay's birthday and the JM stands for Jay Merten. Airplanes from Canada start with C, United Kingdom is G, Spain is EC, Portugal is CS, and Germany is

D. There is a letter for every country in the world.

In General Aviation parking, there are planes from Germany, France, and even a twin engine from the United States. The follow-me truck leaves, and a van pulls up. The female driver greets us and takes us to the General Aviation office. Jay practices his Spanish with the driver. It's late morning and a very sunny day. There never is much shade at an airport for some reason. At the Aviation Office, all we have to do is fill out a form and we're free to go. We head for the main terminal and find a place to rent a cute red compact. We drop our bags in the back of this tiny car and get in. Jay drives the stick shift, and I navigate.

I pull out the guidebook, and Jay says, "You're in charge of our land itinerary."

"Oh, so you trust me after the Faro side trip?" I quip.

"Not really. I just want a rest from planning," Jay barbs back.

He knows we have pretty much the same taste in tourist stops. We drive over winding mountain roads that go up and down and up and down, and I feel a bit woozy. The roads are built right on steep cliffs, so to miss a turn would mean instant death. These switchbacks are quite nerve-wracking, but we manage to sightsee anyway. We observe windmills in all colors and stages of disrepair, the emerald terracing that stripes the farmland, ancient monasteries, the round Bellver castle, and *talyot* ruins: stone structures dating back thousands of years. We taste seafood paella and play with stray *gatitos* hoping to pilfer a bite of our fish. We discover that all the houses have the same forest green shutters, and we marvel at the majesty of the olive trees. We gape at a beaming bride in a breathtaking white gown being photographed at the town's most elegant cathedral, while around the corner a gang of mischievous eight-year-olds steals coins from a public fountain and is lectured sternly by a local policeman. I swim laps in every pool I can find. While here, Jay writes a letter to Bendix King and ships the dead GPS back to the US via DHL shipping service. It costs a small fortune, but he can't find a place to get it fixed in Europe. I need some conditioner for my hair, so I stop in a shop. Amid the Spanish labels, I find *conditionado* and *crème suivant*. Which one do I need? I can't possibly have a conversation with the shop owner in Spanish about what the differences are, so I don't even try. I choose the latter, not knowing whether I'm right or wrong.

After three nights and four days in Palma, we continue on to another beautiful Mediterranean island packed with warm weather, gorgeous beaches, and riveting history: Sardinia. The flight is fast and low-risk compared to the rest of the trip. We can almost be tourists the whole way through the Mediterranean.

We land in Alghero, Sardinia, Italy at a very small airport. Jay rents a blue Panda and we drive to the center of the town of Alghero. We park in a metered space, and the Panda starts honking loudly.

My heart pounds instinctively from the noise. "What in the world?" my reflexes have me say before I think.

Jay studies it, puts the key in the car's ignition, and the noise stops.

A young lady waits to take our parking fee.

"There's a right way and a wrong way to take the key out of the car," says Jay as he emerges from the driver's seat.

We don't have any lira for the meter lady, so I run around the corner to change money, run back, pay the meter lady 1,000 lira, and then we walk around the town.

Alghero was first settled around the 11th century by people from Genova and became an important stop in the

Mediterranean trading route. In 1353, the Catalans took over and it became part of the kingdom of Aragon. Today you can see the Catalan influence in the architecture of the churches, the fortifications, and other buildings as well as the language that the people speak. In Fertilia, we stay at the Hotel Bellavista, a three-star hotel with 70 rooms and beautiful gardens located only a few meters from the sea. There we eat delicious Italian food with a little bit of Italian wine.

In the morning, we take the blue Panda around the Italian countryside to see the very old ruins of a Roman bridge and a very new, beautiful horse farm. We spend all day sightseeing, driving around and staring at the fields, houses, and buildings, and then head to the airport for a 5:00 p.m. takeoff to Malta.

"Do you see that?" Jay nods his head toward the runway as we approach the airport.

"A big jet?" I ask.

"Alitalia jets practicing touch-and-gos," he clarifies. "This airport houses Alitalia's pilots' training base." A touch-and-go is when the airplane lands and then takes right back off instead of taxiing to the hangar.

"That's interesting." It's weird to see a big jet do a touch-and-go, since I have only seen small planes do that as part of a flying lesson.

When we disembark in Malta, it's dark, it's hot, we're tired, and our stress levels are high. We park the airplane, and a van drops us at Arrivals. We breeze through Passport Control, change money, and cakewalk through Customs. We have become experts at conducting airport business quickly and efficiently, even though it is a bit different in each country. We pinpoint the tourist office, obtain a few maps, and rent a white automatic 4-door Hyundai Excel.

"Why don't you drive? It's an automatic," Jay says. It's

not really a question. And he has a point. I can't drive the standard transmissions that are so common to rent in Europe, but I can drive this automatic.

"Are you sure? Then you'll have to navigate," I respond. Even back in Dallas, I learned Jay's ground navigation skills are not his strong suit.

"I'm tired of driving and I'd like a rest," he says nicely and persuasively.

"OK," I say with skepticism. "Get me to Sliema. That's where the hotel is."

I review the car and the road rules of this country in my head. Maltese drivers travel on the left side of the road, and the steering wheel is on the right side. Faced with an overloaded brain from the flight, the new car, the dark, the foreign road rules, and the road signs, which are in Maltese, I slip into the driver's seat. I'm not a happy camper even before I step on the accelerator pedal.

18 July, 1995
Luqa, Malta

*"In your new efforts to be successful, you
will face challenges that don't arise when
you're struggling to be mediocre."*

—*Todd Duncan,*
Time Traps, p. 157.

From the Malta airport, I enter a highway. I have to go fast
so I don't get crunched by the cars behind me. Jay has a map,
but it does no good. He strains to make out a road sign in the
dark. There are no signs to Sliema, but there is a sign to a
nearby town. We reach a traffic circle. By the time we see it,
I can't react fast enough to turn, and I pass it.

"Slow down and watch for the signs!" Jay yells.

"I can't. There are too many cars on my butt!" I yell.

We're both tired and hungry and frustrated.

I suddenly decide to exit the next time I see a traffic circle.
Malta is full of them. Now we're traveling aimlessly on a

narrow road in a village that is not Sliema. The skinny one-way streets curve around, and I think we're traveling over the same roads, in a big loop.

"What are you doing?" Jay yells again.

"Looking for Sliema!" I yell back. "With no help from you."

We're lost. I keep missing turns and moving in circles. I return to the highway. I turn into another town and move in circles. I return to the highway again. I turn into another town and move in circles again. Wash. Rinse. Repeat. Hours pass. We just can't seem to reach Sliema. I have lost confidence.

We see a sign. St. Julian.

It's very late. We agree on a new plan. Let's just find *any* hotel. We search for a hotel here. We can't find anything. Now we're tired, hungry, frustrated, and lost. We've been together constantly for two weeks straight, 24 hours a day, seven days a week. It's too much. I've had enough. The buildup of stress, arguing, constant togetherness, equipment problems, and ground challenges blows up in me all at once. I lose it.

"I'm ready to go home! I don't want any more of this trip!" I shout. Just let me out of the car. I am ready to run away. I love exploring new places, but too much is too much.

Jay loses it too. "Can't you just get back on the highway?"

In the middle of his screaming, I spy a hotel with two stars next to its name. I park in front of it. We enter a dirty hallway. The proprietor has one room left for seven lira. Inside are shreds for towels, a ceiling fan that sways and squeaks, and mattresses as old as this island. It'll have to do.

We both start calming down. Jay is content; I am disgusted, but who can be picky at this point? Fish and chips next door become dinner.

When I lie down on the bed to go to sleep, I can't. I curl up as close to the edge of the bed as I can manage without falling off. I hate being yelled at. It makes me want to go far, far away from where I am now. I feel like escaping. It's my pattern to quit when things go bad.

That may be why Jay and I don't live together, even after a couple of years of dating. I live in my two-bedroom townhouse in North Dallas, and Jay rents a lavishly furnished three-bedroom apartment in a high-rise building about a mile away. When we're not on trips together, we see each other about every three days. Usually Jay comes over to my place, even though it's much smaller and less elegant than his place. I really like having my alone-time. I am very independent. On these trips, it's like we live together and then some. There is so much together-time, it is almost smothering me.

I try to calm myself down. Maybe things will look better in the morning.

In the morning daylight, we regroup. Sliema takes five minutes to locate, and we change hotels, checking into Sliema Chalet Hotel.

This disaster teaches us what works and what doesn't. It works to arrive at a new, strange destination while it is still daylight.

I stop and think about last night again. If that had happened in the cockpit, we'd be dead. We have to pull together as a team if we're going to succeed. Although the traveling has been stimulating, there have been many difficult moments so far. The anticipation and pressure of the upcoming flights scare us both, even if we've done our best to not show it. It takes some honest communication between Jay and me before we pull it together and start acting like a team again.

We try to relax and be tourists for a couple of days longer in this incredibly interesting place of Malta. Stone megaliths date back to prehistoric times: 5,200 BCE. Malta's rich history is comprised of Roman, Byzantine, Muslim, Norman, Spanish, French, and British influences. Strategically located in the Mediterranean, Malta has been desired - and invaded - by just about every nearby country. Today Malta is a republic.

We walk our tails off along St. Elmo's Street to look at St. Elmo's Fort and the War Museum. The fort was built in 1553 and was almost destroyed in the Great Siege of 1565. It was rebuilt two years later and continually modified throughout the centuries. The War Museum is a commemoration to the second Great Siege that occurred during World War II. The most valued artifact is the George Cross, awarded in 1942 to the entire population of the island for their bravery. General Eisenhower's jeep "Husky" is also on display.

"Are you in heaven with all this war stuff?" I ask Jay.

"Absolutely. I find it extremely fascinating and very well-presented," he replies.

A few doors down, we view the 45-minute film, *The Malta Experience*, a multimedia experience of the 7,000 years of Maltese history.

On the other side of the city, the Lascaris War Rooms are the original Royal Air Force fighter control rooms, where the British planned and directed their fight against the Germans and Italians. The name is taken from Grand Master Lascaris. When you walk in, you see lifelike models of uniformed soldiers hunched over planning tables with charts spread all over the tables and walls as if they were in the middle of planning their war movements. In this Command Center, operations were conducted that toppled Rommel's forces in

North Africa, coordinated the invasion of Sicily, and were instrumental in the fall of Mussolini's government. We spend almost an hour immersed in this exhibit, listening to its fascinating story on tape.

Malta has much more history than World War II, so we escape to another part of Valletta to see the Palace of the Grand Masters. The Palace is a very long, pink-bricked building with columns framing the archway around black doors that appear at regular intervals along the side of the building. The building's perimeter contains a fence panel made of short pink concrete columns. Other sides of the building are much more ornate, and the two internal court-yards are filled with statues including one of Neptune with his trident. Black ironwork adorns grills, fences, and the lampposts. Built in 1569, it was later enlarged and now houses much of Malta's government. Its façade consists of marble plaques commemorating milestones in Malta's history.

The city of Valetta is fortified to the gills with war monuments everywhere you turn. We walk and walk and walk along the clean, crowded streets with tourists of every other nationality.

"Let's catch the ferry," Jay says.

"Why?" I ask. There's nothing to see on the other side.

"We can ride it back," he says.

"OK," I say, liking the idea. We ride the ferry across the bay to Sliema and back just because it's there. It's a peaceful break from all the walking we've done. My feet hurt, and I can usually last for miles. The bay water slaps the side of the ferryboat as we cross.

The local luzzu fishing boats are among the most colorful items on the island. Painted in lengthwise stripes of bold colors - vibrant blue, green, red, and yellow - dozens of boats moored next to each other in a line illuminate the harbor. I take lots of pictures. We drive back to Sliema and chow down on pizza at an Italian restaurant. Europeans do not eat their pizza with their hands, so I find myself struggling to cut the pizza with knife and fork to conform to the country's local standards. At the hotel room I sadly throw away my Clusters cereal that I bought in Portugal because it is full of ants. I sleep easily this night, tired from the day's miles of walking.

In the morning we drive to Vittoriosa to see the Maritime Museum.

"I much prefer seeing maritime history to regular war history," I tell Jay as we walk among the exhibits.

"You do?" he asks.

"I'm more fascinated with boats and the sea than I am war strategy, so this museum is interesting to me," I explain. Only open for three years now, it features the actual engine room machinery of the dredger Anadrian, a picture gallery of important marine paintings of the last three centuries, recovered ancient lead anchors, and models of ships.

I think we are on the fast track today, taking in the fishing village of Marsaxlokk in the east and then back to Tarxien where there are temple ruins. West to Mdina, the oldest city in Malta, we walk around this walled city for a while. Then south to Dingli, we walk to the famous cliffs. We hear the muffled booms of artillery practice in the distance. Nearby we visit the Inquisitors Palace, where the doorways to the rooms for prisoners are only about four feet tall. The most interesting story of the whole day is about the domed church of St. Mary in Mosta. On April 9, 1942, a World War II bomb burst through the dome and slid across the floor during a crowded Mass. Two other bombs bounced off the dome and landed in the square. None of them exploded as they all should have. No one was killed. We stop for Cokes in St.

Paul's Bay after driving to Marfa at the northwest tip of the island.

"I really like the mix of cultures in this place. I don't think there's anywhere quite like Malta," I say.

We talk about some of the things we saw today. "Thanks for bringing me here," I say sincerely. To this day, Malta remains one of my favorite places on earth.

"You're welcome," Jay says. "Couldn't do it alone," he adds.

We get lost again on the way back to Sliema. We eat at Krishna Indian restaurant. Our plans are to leave for Crete in the morning.

After breakfast at the hotel, we drive to the airport and turn in the rent car. We both go through Passport Control, X-ray, and Customs stations. We deliver the General Declarations to Customs but apparently we did something wrong upon arrival. They frown at us and let us go anyway. At Gate Five, we wait for the van that will take us to the plane. Jay goes to General Aviation to file the flight plan, get a weather report, and pay the fees. The fuel truck arrives, and I supervise the fueling. I load the airplane and wait for Jay, who has to wait for flight plan approval. In the cockpit, he requests permission to start the engine and to taxi. This is a difference from US flying rules. You don't have to request permission to start the engine, only to taxi. You also have to request permission to descend in this part of the world. In the US, they just tell you. We leave at noon for the three-and-a-half-hour over-water flight to Iraklion, Greece.

In the air over the Mediterranean, Jay points the radar down toward the sea and we spot a tiny blip on the screen. There's no land around, not even a small island. We pass over it and look down. It's a large cargo ship, big enough to register on our radar screen.

The weather is clear and beautiful throughout the flight. During the descent, the cabin's air conditioning kicks in to keep us cool. Upon landing, a follow-me car shows us where to park. A woman directs the plane to an old runway, and we have to park on some white lines. She says a car will come in 15 minutes, then she leaves us. It's hot and sunny. A little later than 15 minutes a car takes us to the airport office where we deliver our General Declaration forms. We follow the signs to Arrivals and stride through Passport Control and Customs. In the police office, they forward our passports to the Passport Office.

We rent a white Panda with a dent and a sunroof and drive to the main airport terminal. There I locate the tourist desk and approach the black-haired man who works there. He gives me a map and suggests a hotel. When I want the map but not the hotel, he takes back the map. He is only interested in his commission. He is not at all helpful.

"We're on our own for a hotel," I declare. "Think we can find one?"

"Sure. Let's go." Jay is always up for an adventure.

We drive to Iraklion which isn't too hard to find despite the Greek signs. I can sound out the Greek words, having learned the Greek alphabet in my college sorority. We find Hotel Kronos in Iraklion for 8,000 *drachma*. It's a little nicer than what we really need, but we check in. Jay and I have always been content with the kind of rooms offered by Motel 6 or Super 8. We find a restaurant and have deliciously different swordfish and a Greek salad with feta cheese.

Jay calls Sharon of Jeppesen DataPlan, a company in California, to find out the status of the permits for the upcoming flights. Commencing in the Middle East, most of the countries require government authorization to land and even to fly over their airspace. If we're not in compliance, we could be shot down. Before we left on this trip, we hired Jeppesen to organize the permits and any requisite ground handling in these foreign countries. We delivered our itinerary to Sharon before we left, and she's been working on our Middle Eastern clearances as the trip has progressed. She tells Jay the Saudi Arabia permit is US $500.00. He instructs her to proceed. We'll be able to fly near Mecca.

In the morning, an eight-page fax from Sharon is waiting for us. We receive permission to fly over Saudi Arabia, Eritrea, and Ethiopia and to land in Egypt, Djibouti, and Kenya, our next three destinations. In Luxor, Egypt, we're also required to have a handling agent, which is someone who will coordinate between us and the airport officials. Sharon includes that information as well.

We drive to a supermarket where I get shampoo, pretzels, and cookies. Jay gets a load of stuff. We try the tourist office but it is closed on Saturday.

Jay looks at me and says, "You've been here before. What should we see?"

"Allow me to be your tour guide for an ancient Minoan palace," I reply in a radio announcer voice.

We drive to the Palace of Knossos and explore the ancient Minoan ruins in the hot and sunny, but bearable, climate.

Jay insists we drive to Plakias, a tiny town in the south where I have also been before - with my ex-husband. Driving in Crete means traversing tiny roads that wind and switchback on mountain cliffs. It's dangerous and there are a lot of traffic deaths on this island. Along the way, we see a sheepherder holding a staff and guiding a flock of about 50 sheep into a valley. The old white buildings glimmer in the sunshine.

We sunbathe on the beaches of Plakias, but not for long because it's too hot outside and the Mediterranean water is too cold. We take off west on the roads marked in red on the map. Some of these are unpaved, but miraculously we never lose our way. The tiny countryside towns are interesting and quaint. We stop at a peaceful, sleepy place called Fournes. We also stop along the way to photograph churches and other scenery. When the road turns to gravel, we ask a local man walking on the road for the way to Omalos. He says "right and down." We do that and amazingly find the town, making no wrong turns. I silently cheer at that little victory. Have we learned something from Malta or is it just easier to get around here?

We stay at Hotel Neos Omalos, a wonderful place with a remote country inn feel. Its white stucco exterior is shaded by tall thick trees. Clay pots filled with bright flowers and plants are scattered along the wide porch. In the wood-paneled dining room of this quaint place, I sip bean soup.

In the morning, we drive to the Samaria Gorge. Jay hikes the entire length and back, and I go about a third of the way, three hours worth of strenuous up-and-down hiking, before turning back. Jay likes to push himself physically. I don't. I read and catch up on my diary in the beautiful sunshine while waiting for him to return. He does, about three hours after my return. We drive to Iraklion and plan to leave Crete in the morning.

We enjoy these Mediterranean places a lot at first, but in Crete the heaviness of what's ahead - flying through Africa and the Middle East - begins to weigh on us. It is difficult for Jay and me to not take our stress out on one another.

Jay and I are both taking risks on this trip, but each of a different kind. For most of the trip, the airplane is uninsured. The insurance resumes after we cross the International Date Line. Jay also must cover any unexpected costs during the trip.

A lack of flying experience comprises my biggest risk. Although I have flown 260 hours in the right seat of the Malibu, if something happened to Jay while the plane was in challenging conditions, I'd be plunged into a life-threatening situation. For someone as independent and stubborn as I am, being so dependent upon another person is a tough place to be. The other risk I am taking is delaying my business. I was just about to start a business before we left; now I will have to delay my plans for several months. This greatly affects my income for this year. So I have a little bit of a financial risk too, although much different from Jay's risk.

Tomorrow we will resume the riskier flights. We don't know what the Malibu's cylinder head temperatures will do in the extreme heat of North Africa, or what will occur over hostile Middle Eastern territories. We haven't repaired our broken equipment. Our relationship is being tested in ways I didn't anticipate. But the journey must continue. Jay is expected to report for volunteer work in Mombasa, Kenya in exactly one week.

6

24 July, 1995
Iraklion, Crete, Greece

The machine does not isolate man from the great problems of nature but plunges him more deeply into them.

—Antoine de Saint Exupéry,
Wind, Sand, and Stars, 1939.

*I*sland hopping in the Mediterranean ends in Crete, and the trip becomes more serious. To benefit from the cooler morning temperatures, we leave Crete as early as possible. Awake at 5:30 a.m., I dress in a short-sleeved light cotton pantsuit with cornflower and white stripes. Jay wears beige shorts, a white polo shirt, and his white wide-brimmed hat. We check out of the hotel, arrive at the airport, and return the rent car before 7:00. At the airport office, Jay obtains a "met," a meteorological update. The international weather forecasts are standardized, but many of the codes are in French, and abbreviations are used for just about everything. For example, BR, short for *brouillard*, means mist. Smoke is FU for *fumée*, and *grêle* (GR) means hail.

Jay completes two carbons of a standardized flight plan form and hands it to the flight controller. The form, created by ICAO, the International Civil Aviation Organization, has been adopted by almost every country except the United States. The controller types the flight data into the computer.

With a little *drachma* left, we pay the landing fees, parking fees, air navigation fees, and whatever else each of these countries can dream up to charge to help cover their airport operation costs. Clearing Customs and Immigration is next, which requires copies of the General Declaration forms we have. A van transfers us to the plane. After we load the bags and arrange the cockpit, Jay radios for permission to start the engine. The flight begins.

The island of Crete shrinks as we leave it behind. Sailboats and ships dot the Mediterranean Sea. From Jay's side of the cockpit, sunlight streams in. The sound of the engine is strong as it climbs.

While we are climbing, the controller notifies us that a live fire military exercise blocks our flight path. To navigate around it, Egyptian air traffic controllers assign a routing nearly 200 nautical miles out of our way. Jay petitions for a higher altitude, and therefore, a more direct route. The heavily-accented controller approves his request. As we climb, the cylinder head gauge edges close to redline.

An airplane's engine shouldn't verge on overheating unless something is wrong. When the Malibu is climbing, too little airflow keeps the engine hot. The design of the cowl, the metal that covers the engine, is so streamlined that it doesn't allow enough air intake for adequate engine cooling. To compensate, pilots can exercise one or more alternatives. They can change the propeller settings so that the engine runs at a higher RPM, letting the propeller take a smaller bite of air, similar to a car running in low gear. They can also adjust the mixture of fuel and air to be a bit on the rich side, which means that there will be excess fuel that won't burn during combustion. This provides cooling as the fuel dissipates the heat of the engine. A third alternative is to climb at a shallow angle. All three of these techniques help to keep the engine cooler.

The indigo of the Mediterranean Sea is soon replaced with bleak brown as we cross from water to land. Overlooking Egypt, miles and miles of sand dominate the scenery. Absent below are roads, buildings, and people. Missing are water, homes, animals, and plants. Only a desolate desert exists. I develop an uneasy feeling as the arid land stretches on. What if we crash? We've stocked a few bottles of water in the emergency kit, but not enough for a place as barren as this. How in the world would a rescue team find us in this isolation? We have our Emergency Locator Transmitter (ELT), but does Egypt have an air rescue team? How would they reach us? When would they start searching for us? How long could we survive in the blistering conditions? For me, I feel more fearful flying over the desert than I do flying over the ocean. In both places, I feel like an insignificant speck.

This part of Amelia Earhart's round-the-world route took her much farther south than the route we chose. She flew from North America to South America, then traveled east to Africa. She crossed the entire African continent, which was much different in 1937 than it is in 1995. One biography, *Amelia: A Life of the Aviation Legend*, described one of the African legs as "one of the most dangerous legs of the journey." Amelia herself described it as "the wildest part of the dark continent" and "Stretches of country barren beyond words, a no-man's land of eternal want." This was the leg between Dakar and Fort-Lamy, just south of Lake Chad. She also described Africa's scenery as barren: "brown plains, bare hills, parched vegetation, and drab dwellings."

I'm warm, unusually so. Born in Dallas, where it surpasses 100°F a few days every summer, I thrive on hot temperatures. I happily set my air conditioning thermostat to a touch above 80°F at home. But today, the cotton fabric of my shirt is starting to stick to my skin.

"Is there a problem with the air conditioning?" I ask.

"It's not working." Jay remarks. This couldn't have happened at a more inappropriate time, I think.

"Take a look at the outside thermometer," Jay says.

"35 degrees Fahrenheit," I read.

"It's nearly 50 degrees hotter than usual. Minus 13 Fahrenheit is a normal reading for 20,000 feet," he notes.

Here above Egypt, it's just plain hot, inside and out. Today's flight will cover 700 nautical miles and will take four to five hours to reach Luxor.

Jay points out the cockpit window at the scene below. "Look at the ground," he tells me.

The arid desert suddenly yields to a distinctive oasis: a long, thin strip of green among the miles of barren brown. As we descend, palm trees, houses, people, buildings, and roads appear below amid the green. A silver ribbon winds through the oasis.

"Know what that is?" he asks me.

It slowly dawns on me. "The Nile River valley."

"That's right," says Jay.

"Cool."

"We're seeing one of the most unique pieces of geography you'll ever see in the world." Jay surmises.

We touch down just after noon in Luxor and park in the middle of a huge empty concrete lot with no shade in sight. The airport building is straight ahead, less than half a kilometer away. It's long and flat, maybe only one story high. The handling agent who we're required to hire, Moataz, greets us in the 43° Celsius heat (109° F), accompanied by someone to carry the luggage and an armed sentry, slinging an automatic weapon, who will guard the plane. I'm wilted even before I climb out of the plane.

"Fill her up," Jay says to Moataz. He arranges it, and a Shell truck with several workers pulls up. All of the workers wear trousers, and a few have long-sleeved shirts on. Perspiring profusely, I can't understand their dress in this heat.

The fuel workers fill each wing full of the blue-tinted avgas 100 LL (low lead), the Malibu's (and most light aircraft's) usual grade of fuel. In Djibouti, the next stop, fuel is unobtainable except in 55-gallon drums, something we'd prefer to avoid if possible. In some countries, avgas is not available at all, which dramatically affects our route planning. Avgas 100/130 octane, colored green, which the Malibu engine prefers, is available on a few stops where our usual gas is not. This latter avgas, not widely offered in the United States, contains too much lead to be environmentally-friendly.

The fuel hose on the Shell truck is equipped with a big metal nozzle. The men unsuccessfully try to squeeze it in the tiny space between the cabin fuel tank's opening and the ceiling of the Malibu. The fumes reek. Everyone is dripping sweat and struggling. My deodorant has stopped working. The fumes and the heat are enough to make a person faint.

Jay crawls inside the stifling cabin to assess the situation. The big fat nozzle won't fit. But we can't just give up. It's not an option. We need fuel; we're on empty. There is no contingency plan available, so we have to keep thinking.

"Jay, we have those plastic hoses we bought in Portland," I remind him. I never did understand how the hoses were going to boost the air conditioning, but now that the air conditioning is broken, the hoses won't be needed for their original purpose.

A plastic hose becomes a makeshift funnel, and the gas pours in. I call out the liters, and all four fuel employees plus Jay work on fueling this plane. The little plane gulps 710 liters. A big grease spot darkens the cabin's beige ceiling from where the men tried to force the nozzle. Jay is woozy from the heat and the fumes. He pulls out several US $100 bills to pay the fuel costs.

To cover expenses like these, Jay brought $9,500.00 in cash. Seven thousand dollars of it is hidden in the lining of the airplane's cabin walls. I brought along $3,000.00, most of it tucked into a money belt I constantly wear beneath my undergarments.

After a couple of hours dealing with the fuel staff at the airport and perspiring all the while in the noontime heat, Moataz, Jay, and I ride a bus from the plane to the terminal. As part of his service package as our handling agent, Moataz will complete all ground handling paperwork. That gives me the rest of the day off. He collects our passports. The two men spend some time discussing the next flight plan. We receive our passports and visas, and an air-conditioned bus is arranged for Jay and me to go to the Winter Palace, a luxurious four-star hotel. The air conditioning in the bus feels like heaven.

"While we're here, why don't you go up to Cairo and see the pyramids?" Jay suggests as we wind through the streets of Luxor. Jay has seen the pyramids outside of Cairo, but I

haven't. I've experienced many natural and manmade wonders, such as the Grand Canyon, the Taj Mahal, Stonehenge,
the Great Wall of China, and Paris's Eiffel Tower. Touring the
pyramids would just about complete my set of world landmarks.

I give him a questioning look, knowing he hates to be left
alone.

"I'd do it if I were you. Who knows when you'll have the
chance again?" he says, as if reading my look.

"Thanks. I'll look into it." Living an extraordinary life is
all about taking opportunity when you can. That's how you
can begin to live bigger than you think you ever could. I'd
love to see both the pyramids and the Egyptian Museum.
That would make for a very successful side trip.

The bus pulls up in front of an ornate pale pink structure
with an elaborate façade, complete with a winding stairway
and terrace. The hotel architecture is Victorian and dates to
1886. Owned by the Sofitel chain, the hotel has a definite
French influence. It's right on the Nile River and next door
to the Temple of Luxor, a major historical attraction.

The elaborate lobby contains what you'd expect a high-
class American hotel to offer: a front desk for check-in, a
concierge desk, an airline desk, a full service restaurant, and
shops. The desk clerk speaks English, and we easily get a
room.

Once inside our air-conditioned room, we relax and cool
down. The room is very nice: a large king size bed with a
fabric-covered headboard, night stand and tables of blond
wood finish, quality draperies, fabric-covered chairs, telephone in the bathroom, paintings, and pale yellow walls. I
remember seeing telephones in the bathrooms in almost
every room I stayed in in China in the late 1980s. It didn't
matter how dumpy the hotel was; there was always a tele-

phone in the bathroom, as if that qualified it to be a world class hotel. This hotel is certainly not dumpy; still, the telephone-in-the-bathroom amenity seems so silly to me.

Jay settles into a nap. I can't sleep during the day, so I go back out into the heat to explore the streets near the hotel. Now, with Jay's encouragement, I locate a travel agent and arrange a commercial flight to Cairo for tomorrow. During my walk, I find a boat cruise that sounds appealing. Jay might want to go on it while I'm away. It might be good for our relationship to spend some time apart after a solid month of being together 24 hours a day, seven days a week, without separation.

Later that evening, Jay and I watch the sun set across the Nile from our hotel room balcony. We savor the peaceful moment.

26 July, 1995
Luxor, Egypt

"To put your life in danger from time to time... breeds a saneness in dealing with day-to-day trivialities."

—Nevil Shute,
Slide Rule: The Autobiography of an Engineer

My Cairo expedition starts in the morning. It's a blistering hot day, so I wear shorts and head for the airport in a taxi that I catch from the hotel. On the flight, I read the Egypt section of the *Lonely Planet* guide to the Middle East. When I reach the paragraph that describes the recommended dress, my heart stops. I completely forget about the Muslim dress that requires head, elbows and knees to be covered. It dawns on me why the men from the airport were covered in long sleeved shirts and long pants. I feel utterly self-conscious on the plane. All I have with me inside my backpack is my camera and water bottle. I can't change my clothes. Today will be terribly painful. I hate going against the culture of a country I am visiting. I don't think I'll have to learn the lesson again.

I carry on despite my wardrobe malfunction. My carefully thought-out plan is to find a hotel near the Egyptian Museum where I can potentially also find a pyramids tour. At the Cairo airport, I search for the tourist office, seeking information. I cannot find it.

"Where is the tourist office?" I ask someone.

A man points to a building. I follow his direction and end up at a tour desk, which is not the same as a tourist office.

I stop a policeman. "Where is the tourist office?" I repeat. He directs me to the tourist police. But that's not what I want either. I'm feeling hopeless standing there in my shorts, and the day has barely started. Sometimes I feel it's harder for a woman traveling alone. It's much easier in Europe, but Egypt is definitely not Europe.

I finally stumble into someone who has a map that I can look at. I find that the Nile Hilton is right next to the museum. Perfect. That's all I need to know.

I try to hire a taxi to take me to the Nile Hilton. I walk toward the taxis, about four of them, all with men shouting at me in broken English to come with them. The four male drivers bargain with me, beckon me to come with them, competing for my fare, and I don't know what the right thing to do is. One of them grabs my suitcase and takes off with it. I run after it. This is freaking me out. Where is the orderly queue? Who is first? Who will be cheapest? Who will be safe? I'm quite unnerved.

A policeman intervenes yet again and waves me into a taxi. I get in, still not knowing who to trust. At the airport exit, I have to sign my name on a form. As soon as we exit the airport, the taxi driver tries to convince me to drive around with him all day.

"I take you on tour of Cairo," he begs. I try to stay busy viewing the sights. After all, I'm here to relax and be a tourist.

"No, thank you. Nile Hilton, please," I say firmly, but as nice as I can for the fifteenth time.

Inside the Hilton, I find an American Express office. They have a half-day afternoon tour of the pyramids called "Pyramids of Giza and Sphinx." Perfect, I think. My plan is finally working. I happily sign up. With the day's arrangements made, I can now relax a little. When I'm alone in a foreign country, I never completely relax: I arm myself with what I call my "street smarts." I'm constantly aware of what's going on around me, where I am, and what the threats are. I just do this instinctively. I also maintain an air of confidence, no matter how scared I feel. Thieves and others usually don't come after confident people; they come after weak people.

I walk over to the Egyptian Museum and purchase a ticket. Both my camera and I need a ticket to get in. I don't think I've ever run across that before. Inside the museum, the artifacts, hieroglyphics, tombs, treasures, and mummies mesmerize me for hours. I am fascinated by how well-preserved these objects are after thousands of years. It's one of the best museums I've ever explored. I feel much safer here than in that morning's circus, plus I don't feel as self-conscious of my dress any more. No one has said anything or given me dirty looks.

In the afternoon, I proceed to the designated meeting place and join the tour. An Arab couple, the guide, the bus driver, and I sit in the bus. I cover my exposed knees with my red backpack. The bus driver takes us to Giza, a plateau about six miles west of Cairo, and to the pyramids. In

English and Arabic, the guide spews out facts and figures about the unique structures. We drive by three of the pyramids, Cheops, Chephren, and Mykerinos, and I exit the bus to explore one of them. I step down in my tennis shoes, and the hot sand shifts underneath my feet as I step. The heat is ruthless. I cling tight to my water bottle. Gigantic red ants scramble over the sand where I walk. An unhappy-looking camel with a beautifully colored saddle kneels in anticipation of a passenger. Its owner wants money. Another man wants my water bottle. I keep it to myself. Still another man approaches me and says, "Are you as beautiful as your husband?" I say nothing, dumbstruck at this line. It ends up that he wants to marry me for a visa to live in the United States. I often thought that somehow, when someone did ask me to marry him that it would be different from what I just experienced. So much for having great expectations of the opposite sex.

In bright gleaming sunlight, the huge sand-colored triangles point to the azure sky. Two of the pyramids are made with limestone casing, and the smaller one is made with granite casing. As I get closer, I see that each stone block is huge. I crawl down into the dusty shaft of one and smell urine. Something this old, over 4,500 years, is probably going to smell bad, I think.

I am a bit surprised to see that the pyramids, although big, are not as big as I thought they would be. It could be my experienced traveler's eyes. The tallest of these three pyramids is 479 feet. That's less than half the height of the Eiffel Tower and forty percent of the height of the New York's 1931-built Empire State Building. Although they're no longer the tallest structures in the world, they are certainly among the most massive. The Great Pyramid of Cheops, named for a king of the fourth dynasty, covers 13 acres and is estimated to contain three million stone blocks, each weighing two and a half tons. All of this is located in what used to be the city of Memphis, the power center of ancient pharaohs and kings.

According to the guide, the regal Sphinx possesses the body of a lion, representing strength, and the head of royalty. Its face is supposedly Chephren's, the king who built the second pyramid of our tour. The Sphinx is made out of limestone, and the blocks weigh up to 70 tons, much larger than the blocks that compose the pyramid. It's the same age as the pyramids. However, some experts think the Sphinx is older. It originally had a cobra headpiece and a beard, but these pieces have been removed over time.

There is much wild speculation about the pyramids. From questions about their cosmological importance and mathematical significance to who built them, why, and when, crazy theories abound. I sure don't have the answers. The guide says the Sphinx was used solely to prepare Chephren for his death.

We continue the tour to a papyrus factory, the final stop. The papyrus plant grows in meter-deep water along the Nile and can grow as tall as five meters (roughly sixteen feet). It's not a coincidence that "papyrus" and "paper" sound similar. Egyptians made paper from papyrus thousands of years ago. A factory demonstration shows us how they cut, flattened, dried, wet, and pressed the papyrus plant into paper. After the demo, we have a chance to buy papyrus souvenirs. Each papyrus print tells a long story and has deep meaning. I choose one with a figure that looks like Cleopatra.

At sunset, I board an Airbus A320 jet back to Luxor. A business man approaches me and asks for my water bottle. Why does everyone want my water bottle today? When I look perplexed, he explains he is in the business and would like to have the label from my Greek-manufactured bottle because he hasn't seen it before. No problem. That I can do. It's the first reasonable request I've had from someone today.

In Egypt, I feel like everyone wants something from me, often in return for nothing. That makes me feel a bit uncomfortable. I wish I knew more about why this happens.

Later, entering the hotel room, I can't wait to greet Jay. "Hi! How was your day?"

"Great. I joined the boat tour that you found," he says. "It was nice. Did you see the pyramids?"

Part of me can't believe Jay did something I suggested. "Yes, and I'm glad to be back," I say with a frown on my face. "The day was a wonderful success, but I felt hassled the whole time."

Most of the time, I prefer voyaging alone. It forces me past my comfort zone to meet strangers, and I am able to more deeply absorb the culture I am visiting. But today was more challenging than usual.

In the morning, Jay and I take part in a Luxor West Bank tour that requires a taxi, a ferry, and a bus ride. We see tombs, statues, and ruins. Fascinating hieroglyphics, Tutankamen's tomb, Hatshepsut's palace ruins, and King Ramses's history fill our day. Not at all the type for organized tours, Jay acts fairly civilized today. We get along better than we have in weeks. We have both benefited from our short time away from each other. I don't know any relationship that can weather as much companionship as we have had recently without a respite.

On the morning of our departure from Luxor, we don our "uniforms" for the first time: dark trousers with belts, white shirts, and epaulets on our shoulders. Jay sports four gold stripes on his epaulet; I wear three so as not to outrank his male ego. I don't know our levels; we simply bought the outfits at Sporty's Pilot Shop.

We commissioned crew cards from a company called Baseops International. I borrowed Jay's tie, smoothed my thick hair, and posed for the card's photo. Neither of us smiled to make it look more authentic. The card shows the picture, the label "Crewmember," my name, birthday, weight, height, eye color, hair color, expiration date, and authorized signature. Jay's picture looks more professional with his short gray hair and serious look. Now that we've entered Africa and are approaching the Middle East and Asia, we believe that the uniforms and crew cards will expedite our dealings with airport personnel.

At 7:00 a.m. at the Luxor airport, the x-ray machine is not operating. We wait for airport personnel as both Jay's anxiety and the temperature rise. We want to depart as early as possible to avoid the extreme African afternoon heat. Amelia's challenges were the same as ours: heavy fuel loads and extreme temperatures. To avoid the heat, she often scheduled 6:15 a.m. takeoffs.

Moataz presents Jay with a huge bill for services and fees. Jay peels off several US $100 bills and hands them to Moataz. The men complete their paperwork, and Jay turns his focus to the airplane. He checks the oil and adds a quart. We climb in the stifling hot Malibu and buckle up in the leather seats, feeling more hot than official in our dark long pants. Avgas fumes saturate the cabin; I wrinkle my nose as if that will help. We start the engine, taxi to the runway, and depart for Djibouti a little after 8:00 a.m. with full tanks, empty pockets, and no air conditioning. The hum of the engine pierces the otherwise silent sky.

Djibouti is a tiny country across the Red Sea from Yemen. It gained its independence from France in 1977. A prime trading destination throughout history, Djibouti enjoys a wonderful harbor and is surrounded by Eritrea, Ethiopia, and Somalia. Its association with its Arabian neighbors dates back thousand of years. This area was the first in Africa to adopt Islamic practices.

To reach Djibouti entails six hot hours and more than 1,000 nautical miles of flight. With no working GPS, we rely on VOR navigation. For each VOR waypoint on our flight plan, we dial the pre-assigned frequency into our radio to see if we can attract the ground signal.

Over Egypt, Sudan, and Eritrea, many of the VORs are not working. This reduces our ability to know exactly where we are and to navigate to where we need to go. Is it because of the many wars in this part of the world, I wonder? Or is it because the infrastructure is not maintained? I've observed several African and Asian projects where foreign aid delivers new roads and buildings, but no plan follows for subsequent maintenance and repair. Countries like Eritrea must wrestle with food shortages and starving families. How can it afford to repair its airport system if it can't feed its residents? If I were a government official, I'd probably spend money on food instead of aviation infrastructure. Shortchanging either problem is bound to lead to death for many. With no clear solutions, these ethical dilemmas whirl around in my head.

Near Eritrea, Jay tries calling Asmara Control on the radio and gets no answer. After a while, he gives up. Is the air traffic employee taking a break? Is he out sick today? Is the position open? How will we calculate our location with no radio contact and so few working VORs?

I'm no longer keen on flying over Africa, yet we've only just begun. I'm frustrated too - it's hot, our equipment is broken, the cylinder head temperature still borders redline, and now no one answers the radio. My fear increases as it dawns on me that we are taking much greater risks than I originally calculated. This trip is simply harder than I thought it would be.

Amid my fears and frustration, I realize something. Any dream worth doing should be hard. It should be a little frustrating, scary, and challenging. The whole point of an adventure like this is to learn as much as we can and mature mightily from it. In order for our souls to grow, whatever task we tackle must be *difficult*.

My mind comes around to accept my circumstances, no matter how hard. After all, I got myself into this. I decide there's no place else I'd rather be right now than here. It's just a more powerful way of thinking, being in the moment and enjoying it, than the alternative of worrying about what *could* happen.

Jay points the weather radar down to see if he can make out the coastline of the Red Sea, much like he did to find the Azores islands. The edge of the Red Sea should display when we approach it. According to the chart, Mecca is due east, across the Red Sea.

A few hours later, about 80 nautical miles from Djibouti, radio contact resumes. The controller's African accent is difficult to understand, but at least someone knows where we are. We spot the Red Sea, the Djibouti harbor, and the airport. We arrive around 3:00 p.m. local time, parking between a Russian plane and one from the United Nations.

Osman, an airport employee originally from Ethiopia, greets us with an unusual welcome. "We know you just got raked by Egyptian authorities. Welcome to Djibouti, the country with no hassles and no huge fees." His English is excellent. With high, full cheekbones, Osman's brown eyes sparkle when he smiles. His dark curly hair and beard hold a touch of gray. He helps us through every step, from Immigration all the way to booking our hotel. He makes us feel unusually comfortable in such a foreign place.

The streets of Djibouti hold many surprises. Army-green

uniformed troops from the French Foreign Legion stride among the natives. Women cover their heads and bodies with peach, red, blue, and purple robes that look similar to Indian saris. Men wear short sleeved solid-color shirts and slacks in blues, tans, and whites. Many people hum or sing as they walk through town. Tourists are infrequent here; relief workers are common. Most of the foreigners, of European and Indian heritage, own shops, restaurants, or hotels in town. The official languages are French and Arabic. About ten percent of the population are nomads in the bush.

The water shortage is acute. To do our part, we avoid long showers and don't launder clothes. One day the water is cut off all afternoon. This leaves no place to go to the bathroom; you just have to wait. Electricity is intermittent and unreliable and goes off in the mornings. A guy on the street solicits 500 Djibouti francs to buy *powdered* milk for his baby. I've been approached by many beggars around the world, but no one has ever asked me for powdered milk. I give money to organizations, but never to individuals, and I don't break that rule today. Signs warning of the dangers of *SITA* (AIDS) are posted sporadically around the city center. The white concrete buildings badly need a paint job.

The desperation and poverty of this place are frightening. Coming from the United States where there is so much abundance, the scarcity in this place is hard to take. Choices are few here. Whenever there are few choices, discontent thrives. Djibouti is such a new country. A republic, it gained its independence from France only recently, in 1977. The French settled here in the 19th century after the Suez Canal was started.

We try to sign up for a tour, but the tour guides are busy with another group. Osman offers to escort us around town. He meets us wearing a thin white cotton shirt, navy trousers, and leather sandals. In the hot sun, the three of us saunter around the market, the bus station, and the shops. The streets are filled with the honking horns of busses, motorcycle engines being gunned, muffled conversations, and sandals shuffling from place to place. The market stalls consist of wooden lean-to's with sheet metal roofs. Bunches of bananas hang from the stalls. The fruits and vegetables for sale in the market likely came from trading with other countries as the climate here is arid. The town smells of sweet fruit, car exhaust, and human perspiration.

When we walk alone, beggars approach us and vendors vie for our attention and a piece of our pocketbook. When Osman accompanies us, no one hassles us. Osman is well-respected. Plus, he knows just about everyone. His cousin, a nurse, greets us. Several airport employees say hello. The head of Air Traffic Control rushes by. All 250,000 people in Djibouti must be acquainted with or related to one another.

Through our explorations, we find out Cokes are 600 Djibouti francs in the restaurants, 150 Djibouti francs at the kiosk across from the hotel, and 50 Djibouti francs around the corner in the natives' neighborhood. Djibouti used to be home to 84 bars, but the government shut all but five of them down. Osman has aspirations for the future. He wants to take a correspondence course to learn about computers. With the Internet, he may be able to. Jay encourages him and emphasizes the value of an education.

Osman shares his thoughts about spirituality as we walk in the streets. "Religion is like a diamond with many facets. Each facet symbolizes a different religion, its beliefs, its rituals, and its people. You can look at each side of the diamond and see each of the different religions in the world. Each facet is joined to the center of the diamond. You can look through the facet to see the inside of the diamond. In that center, inside the diamond, is God. All religions worship the same God. It's one God. They might not think they do, but they do," Osman says.

At sunset, men haul in their fishing nets and tally their catches. A few sailboats are moored in the Gulf of Aden. The sun-faded aqua, mint green, and white Djibouti flag waves in the wind in front of the Palace of the President. Later that night, Osman drops by our hotel and offers Jay his medals that he earned during the Gulf War. I give Jay a questioning look, but Jay is flattered and takes them. Osman wants us to remember him.

From Djibouti, the departure is easy and we head for Mombasa, Kenya. After a slow, hot climb, we voyage across endless stretches of Ethiopian and Kenyan desert. Dire Dawa is one of the first checkpoints.

An hour and a half into the flight, no one is home. No other airplanes are in the vicinity. No air traffic controllers hear us. We can't pick up any working VOR signals. All navigation and radio contact is gone. We are flying blind. Jay dials in the squawk code of 7600, an emergency code denoting loss of radio contact.

This is no time to stray from the flight path. It's a really bad time to be without a GPS. All around us, the countries demand overflight permits. In addition, a pilot must precisely follow the prearranged flight path. One year, the Ethiopian government shot down a US-registered Learjet containing two European citizens who flew too close to Adwa, Ethiopia and entered a no-fly zone. They were both killed.

We don't want to be shot down or accidentally fly into a restricted or military area. But how will we know? We can rely on the charts only so far. There are no visual clues, only a vast brown wasteland below. I was tense over Egypt and

Sudan, but now I am really anxious.

Amelia and Fred, Amelia's navigator, had similar problems finding landmarks over northern Africa as they flew. With poorly developed charts in 1937, Fred found the barren land of Africa much more difficult to traverse than the oceans. I feel the same way. Although we have better charts, if all the ground systems are broken, they won't do us much good.

For two hours we fly this way, sort of pointing south, making an educated guess, and hoping for the best. Jay is less nervous than I am. The way he controls his fears is by thinking about alternative choices. "If this happens, I can do A or B, then C." If he knows he has an out, he is not nervous. Right now, we can keep tuning in different frequencies. We can look at the ground for visual clues like runways. We can listen for airplanes in the region that can relay our position. And we can navigate using all of the available alternatives on board.

We tune in the WAJIR waypoint, a VOR, which usually relays the distance and direction to the station. This time, Jay receives the distance from the station, but not the direction *to* the station. Our navigation computer can determine the speed we're flying to the station, so Jay improvises to find the distance. He homes in on WAJIR by altering his course slightly to maximize the speed readout.

"According to the calculation, we are 20 miles ahead of where we guessed we were," surmises Jay.

"Good job, Captain," I encourage. It's really good considering even the smallest wind could blow us off course.

He spots a runway, a signpost for us. I spot another one. We locate them on the chart. From this information, we adjust our southerly bearing.

A VOR signal at Garissa allows us to confirm our position. South of Garissa, a Uganda Air Force pilot relays our location. We have just crossed the Equator. After Garissa, we receive the Mombasa waypoint. We can relax a little since we know we're over Kenya, but not for long.

The Mombasa air traffic controller wants us to perform a full ILS (Instrument Landing System) approach, requiring a maneuver called a procedure turn. It has us reversing course, never a productive use of fuel. Jay grumbles. It's sunny, and he can see the runway, but he complies and maneuvers the plane along the prescribed path. We touch down and taxi toward a marshaller holding up orange paddles in each hand.

The marshaller guides us to temporary parking for the Malibu and accompanies us to the terminal. He phones the Lighthouse for Christ Eye Center, where we plan to settle, and arranges for someone to pick us up. We pop into the airport office.

"We're going to be here for a month doing humanitarian work. Where do you suggest we park?" Jay inquires.

The officials say they will look into it for us and get back to us. For now, Jay parks it in the General Aviation lot next to ten or so other Pipers and Cessnas.

After clearing Immigration, Frank, the Center's director, and Onesman, a driver, greet and collect us. Frank, an American, looks slight next to Onesman's tall build. While in Mombasa, Jay will perform surgeries for this missionary organization. At the director's request, he and I will reside on their grounds in separate quarters since we are not married. Both Jay and I think the arrangement is quaint, but we conform since they are our hosts.

The streets of Mombasa are chaotic. Onesman skillfully dodges goats, potholes, and pedestrians on our way to the Center. Houses and buildings are surrounded by stone fences topped with broken glass, designed to cut anyone who tries to scale the fence.

The Lighthouse for Christ Eye Center compound is guarded by armed men with dogs. A fence surrounds the property, even the side that faces the harbor. At dusk, the front gate is securely locked, and dozens of floodlights illuminate the driveway. There is an emergency alarm buzzer over my bed. The whole city seems to scream, "KEEP OUT!" I wonder what the residents are so fearful of. Are they afraid of each other?

1 August, 1995
Mombasa, Kenya

"Man must rise above the Earth - to the top of the atmosphere and beyond - for only thus will he fully understand the world in which he lives."

—*Socrates*

As the word spreads that there is an ophthalmologist in the house, business at the Lighthouse for Christ Eye Center grows. Located on a 25-foot cliff overlooking Mombasa Harbor, the compound consists of several buildings: a waiting area, a surgery room, upstairs offices, and several small houses. Tropical plants and palm trees accent the white stucco buildings with shingled roofs. The houses that line the back of the property host a spectacular view of the harbor and the coastline across the water. The compound is located about a mile from the city center.

I reside in the pastor's two-story house while he and his

family are away on vacation in the United States. Frank instructs me on how to lock up the house, secure the windows, and turn on the outside lights. It's a multi-step procedure that Frank takes very seriously and leaves me feeling like I shouldn't trust this place. Frank and his wife, Phyllis, dwell in another house; Jay settles in a room one story below Frank and Phyllis; and Roberta and her two kids inhabit the other end of the compound in a house with multiple bedrooms. An American, Roberta lives in Germany, is married to a German, and received her medical schooling there. New at surgery, she hopes Jay will guide her through several cases while he's here. A tall brown-eyed brunette, Roberta is jovial and worldly.

Jay and I plan to stay the entire month of August. The other residents' terms range from a six-month visit to a year-long accommodation.

Each morning before dawn, I wake to the chants of a muezzin. At 4:30, he calls to Muslims over a loud speaker that is wired to a city-wide sound system. For an hour, he chants a stream of prayers, his voice lilting in a somewhat addictive, soothing melody. I unlock the house before 7:00 every morning, and Jay joins me for breakfast before starting rounds. Since his quarters do not contain a kitchen and mine do, he is "allowed" to visit me in the morning. I make tea by boiling the local water. When I pour it in the cup, a film appears on top of the liquid. It doesn't look safe to drink, but I do anyway. I fix breakfast, which ranges from bread with jam to fruit and cereal.

One morning, he tells me a secret. "Did you know that Frank wanted you to stay in a hotel instead of on the grounds?"

"Because we're not married?" I ask.

"I guess."

"Hmmm. I could do that but I'd rather not. It would cost me about two grand. Plus I'd be bored. What would I do all that time?" I ask. Already, I feel very unwelcome in this place.

Throughout our stay, I make several trips to the grocery to buy drinks, food for breakfast, and snacks. One time at the market, I need bananas.

I pick out a bunch of bananas and hold it up. "How much?" I ask the vendor.

He tells me a high price.

I set the bunch down and say, "Thank you."

I walk to another vendor across the market and select another bunch.

"How much?" I ask.

She quotes me a high price.

I lay the bananas back on the table and smile.

At the third vendor, I have better luck. The price is reasonable.

When I return from the market, I mention my price woes to Nora, a worker at the Center.

"That is terrible," she exclaims. "Let me go for you next time."

"No, you have so much other work to do. It's OK," I say. "It was an interesting experience. It was my first time to learn how discrimination feels."

Each evening, at 10:30 p.m. sharp, African and Indian music waft loudly from the bay. It's coming from a dhow owned by the Tamarind restaurant that sails in the bay next to the Center. The restaurant is straight across the bay on the other side.

All day long, Jay treats patients, coaches Roberta, and handles the more difficult cases himself. The Christian staff works with the Muslim community to tell them about

Christianity and to try to convert them. While in the waiting room, patients listen to the story of Jesus narrated in Swahili on a closed-circuit TV. Surgery is not begun until the doctor or scrub nurse leads the team in prayer. On the grounds is a chapel, where the Bible is quoted, a choir sings, and Christian services are conducted. The Eye Center is only one of dozens of Lighthouse for Christ "churches" around Kenya.

I have no problem with Christians offering eye care to Muslims. But when patients are forced to view a video about Christ's birth before their doctor's appointment; well, to me, that's just inappropriate. It stifles a person's freedom, in trade for health care, which, if offered, should be given with no strings attached.

I wish to support Jay, so I don't verbalize my thoughts. But I also decide to myself that I don't want to be part of one of these mission programs again. When a Muslim is converted to Christianity in this part of the world, his family disowns him. All of this makes me feel very uncomfortable and internally conflicted. I bottle this up, playing the nice girlfriend and the polite guest as if nothing is wrong.

At 10:00 every morning, milk tea is prepared in traditional Indian style and served in British style. Some days, I join the staff for this sweet morning treat. At 5:30 p.m. on certain days, John, one of the ministers, holds a prayer meeting in the chapel. Christian music sung in Swahili wafts from the building. At 6:30 p.m. daily, the muezzin starts his chants over the city loud speaker, often drowning out the music in John's prayer meeting.

When Frank discovers I know something about computers, he drags out an old Atari from a closet, the staff sets up a makeshift classroom, and I teach three classes a day to them. I'd never seen a computer without a hard drive. The Atari was manufactured circa 1985, when operating system software was loaded via a floppy drive. I teach myself from the manual right before I teach the class.

"Can I be your assistant?" Thula, Roberta's daughter, asks. The brown-haired, brown-eyed nine-year-old is tall for her age and lanky like her mother. Fluent in English and German, she is bright and learns fast.

"Absolutely. That would be very helpful," I encourage.

On the first day of computer class, Thula designs a sign for the classroom door all of her own initiative. The staff creates a chalkboard from a rough piece of black wood. Thirty people attend the first week: office workers, drivers, maintenance men, clergy, and housekeepers. Thula hands out a pad and a sharpened pencil to each student. She also supplies the teacher with chalk and erases the blackboard. I lecture the participants on the parts of the computer and how to use the mouse.

The students take turns practicing on the lone computer. The clickety-clack of keys is slow and sure as each student tries out the machine and builds their confidence as they complete the task. One day, we type a complete sentence in a word processor program, another day we cut and paste, the next lesson we learn to copy files, and after that we take on italicizing, bolding, and underlining words. The power goes out one day, so I lecture for a while and let the class out early. During private lessons, I teach spreadsheet and database skills to a few of the office workers. Once, arriving late for a private class with a new student, I find Thula has already started the class without me, gesturing and reciting, "Input - Process - Output," the same lesson I taught the first day. I get a kick out of this; it cracks me up and I giggle about it for the rest of the day. I don't have the privilege of being around children much back home.

As the class unfolds, I discover I have much to learn as a

teacher. It's not only my first time teaching, but it's in a different culture and country. I love the idea of teaching, but I'm not certain which topics would be most practical for the workers here. Most importantly, I realize I lack the patience and persistence that the students need. The students are wiser than the teacher. They reflect my behavior back to me so I can learn from this experience. A few people excel and are able to write complete letters using the computer. Many others drop out because the learning curve is too steep.

Jay endures some difficult days in the clinic. One day, 76 patients sign up, seeking medical attention. He works until past 6:30 that night. A few of the surgeries develop complications that Jay must confront. He sees his first ever AIDS patient. The lady, whose husband left her, wears a turquoise veil to cover her eye which contains a fungating tumor. Jay tries to provide the best care that he can to each patient.

One day, Jay says, "I'd like you to come into the surgery room and watch a case."

"Wow. That'd be cool," I reply. "I can take pictures of you in action." I'd never be able to enter an operating room in the United States as an observer, so this is a once-in-a-life-time opportunity. I wear a mask, cap, and gown and enter the OT (operating theatre) with my camera to document cases. Peering through the microscope, I watch Jay cut the eye and express, or remove, the cataract from the patient who is awake, but anesthetized locally. I snap shots from all angles, being careful not to blind Jay or any of the staff with the flash. The surgery is an amazingly precise and detailed procedure on one of the most precious organs of our body. It's a real miracle operation - taking someone who is blind from cataracts and enabling them to see after 20 minutes of surgery.

It's no coincidence that medicine and flying attract the

same type of person. Both professions require years of training to learn difficult tasks that must be executed perfectly.
They require constant practice to keep skills sharp and current. Both professions have dire consequences for failure or
even for substandard performances. No emotion is allowed.
If an emergency arises, the person can't panic; they have to
move into checklist mode and do what it takes to resolve the
problem.

Jay and I eat dinner together almost every night. Besides
breakfast, it's the only time we see each other. For that reason, we get along fairly well with a few exceptions. Jay
wants me to accompany him daily to the airport to check the
plane. Although Mombasa houses many General Aviation
planes, it feels risky to keep the Malibu here. Construction at
the airport leaves the parking area unlit, and there's a gaping
hole in the airport perimeter fence anyone can pass through.
In this part of the world, Jay's plane is uninsured. Often,
radios and GPS devices are stolen from planes. Two planes
have recently been broken into. At some airports, thieves
drain petrol from the gas tanks. One pilot forgot to check his
fuel level before takeoff and crashed to his death.

A few days after we arrive in Mombasa, two airport
employees visit us at the Eye Center to let Jay know they
have found private parking for his plane at a very high price:
US $700. This offer makes Jay question the safety of his plane
even more than before and worries him a great deal.
Bridgette, a Swiss lady who flies missionaries around Kenya,
says it's safer to stay in the General Aviation airport parking.
During our time in Mombasa, Jay stops at the airport every
other day to examine the Malibu. Since I have classes, I cannot accompany him to the airport. Many days, I feel unwell
and need to lie down. I only make a few trips with him, and
he doesn't appreciate that.

Often in the evenings, an event is planned with the others living in the compound. One night, our group caravans to the Whistling Pines restaurant that serves a traditional Swahili meal of chicken, greens, potatoes, beans, and rice. They don't just feed people, however. A few feet from the dinner tables is a pond - filled with crocodiles. The after-dinner show at this restaurant consists of watching staff feed the crocodiles. The crocodiles have to work for their food. Skinned, beheaded chickens dangle 15 feet above the crocodiles, who lunge up and sink their teeth into them. You can hear the surge of water as they jump, then the snap of the jaws closing on the chicken.

I ask Jay, thinking about our two most touristy shows so far, "Which do you like better: the belly dancer from Tanger or this croc show?"

He gives me a look.

Some days for dinner we wander around the corner to a nearby restaurant; other days we drive around town in a broken down Peugeot truck, one of the Center's spare vehicles. The truck is greasy inside, there are parts stacked on the passenger's floor, and the passenger door doesn't open. When rolling down the window on the driver's side, the handle comes off in Jay's hand. But the truck runs and gives us freedom to see Mombasa. Delicious Indian food with curries, lentils, chutneys, rice, and *naan* bread is the predominant dish in Mombasa.

Roberta and Phyllis arrange for Nora and Doreen, local housekeepers, to cook a few of the evening meals. They graciously consider Jay's and my dietary restrictions of eating only fish and vegetarian food. We are served delicious fish curry, vegetable *pulao*, and a lentil curry with *chapatis*. I sit with Nora, from the Seychelles, one afternoon to learn how to reproduce her delicious, authentic recipes. She talks about her home and shows me a *coco de mer*, which is a double coconut in one shell, that she has kept for a souvenir.

One evening, we visit a missionary couple associated with the Center. Gary and Jean have adopted two African-American kids, Nathan and Hannah. Their house is across the bay from the Center, and they have lived there four years. For their protection, they utilize a guard, attack dogs, an alarm system, and a wire fence around the property. Other places sport eight-foot high walls surrounding their places. I keep wondering what everyone is so fearful of, so I finally ask.

"What are you protecting yourself from?"

Gary says, "Mostly robbers. People can't own guns here, but they do have knives."

Jean adds, "A missionary couple was killed here just last year."

I nod in understanding.

Gary works to convert the Muslims to Christianity and has a Sunday school and a church where he is pastor. Both kids are eerily well-behaved, and Nathan draws rockets all night. Later, Jay takes him up in the Malibu for a short local flight.

The most memorable meal during our stay is a lobster dinner at the Tamarind Restaurant. Just the two of us, Jay and I enjoy a wonderful view of the harbor. On the balcony, looking up at the stars, we can see the Southern Cross, a marvel of the Southern Hemisphere. Jupiter shines brightly inside the constellation Scorpio.

Many activities keep us busy. One day, it is horseback riding with the kids, Thula and Nathan. Thula is decked out in English riding gear. We drive to a place in the country which has several horses and a guide. Thula, Nathan, the guide, and I take a leisurely ride into the countryside, then come back and ride around the arena for a while. Jay stays on the ground and snaps a bunch of pictures. The smells of the horses, the grasses, and the leather saddles flood my senses with memories of growing up on a ranch. The clop-clop of the horses hooves settles into a familiar rhythm. As a teen, I trained horses and taught horseback riding. My instincts kick in naturally, and I give Nathan and Thula some pointers.

The ride brings me peace for an hour. The guide says I should get a job teaching horseback riding here. I consider it fleetingly. I've always wanted a job in a country other than the United States, but have never been able to find one that matches the cost of living I needed. Amelia had a love for horses as well. She used to show up for flying lessons wearing her riding breeches.

One Saturday night, we holiday at Two Fishes Hotel, a place where missionaries relax from their work. Jay and Roberta windsurf, and I lazily enjoy the beach.

One weekend, encouraged by Jay, I travel alone to Lamu on a tourist package. I board a Czechoslovakian LET 410 with fifteen or twenty Africans and watch the two pilots carefully as they maneuver the small plane up to all of 7,500 feet altitude. I feel a little nervous flying as a passenger in this plane. Perhaps it's not the plane at all but the people and strange places that have me a bit apprehensive. When I arrive, I find it charming.

The unique island of Lamu is packed with 17,000 people, 10,000 cats, 3,000 donkeys, one Land Cruiser, and no cars. One veterinarian has made it his life's work to neuter as many cats as he can. He can distinguish the neutered ones by a notch he inscribes on their ears. When I admire the donkeys, my guide laughs at me and asks, "Why do you like the donkeys?"

"I don't know. I like animals." I'm not too sure of my answer.

The Lamu people learn Swahili and the Koran in Arabic. My guide insists on teaching me Swahili. The town dates to the 14th century and contains 26 mosques and one Christian church. Residents' houses are very private. Wives and daughters in Lamu are not permitted to answer the door; only the husband and eldest son can receive visitors. If no man is home, the door goes unanswered. Is there really such a place in the 20th century? (I keep the thought to myself.)

The guide is nice, and I feel more comfortable here than in Cairo for some reason. I just don't feel as threatened. I spend the night in the Lamu Palace Hotel where I am served a delicious local fish dish with a wonderfully exotic mix of African and Indian spices. The following day, I ride in a dhow, an Arab sailing ship rigged with a triangular sail. I love the feel of sailing: how the boat rhythmically moves with the water. It's quite a treat to enjoy this hot, sunny day on such an authentic and unusual vessel. I am the only tourist on the boat. My crew is friendly and talks about sailing races, the local gossip, their work, and their families. I listen, completely fascinated by all. They show me pictures of their racing sailboat, complete with skull and crossbones adorning its sail. I don't think I've ever seen one except in cartoons. On the way back "home," encouraged by the other passengers, I ride in the copilot seat of the 12-seat Cessna plane. I watch his GPS with envy.

Back in Mombasa, I start driving lessons. Outside of the US, most rent cars have standard transmissions instead of automatic. Although I learned to drive an H-pattern in a jeep from my dad when I was 13, I have lost my timing after nearly 25 years of driving automatic cars. I can practice here where the lessons are roughly one dollar an hour and can be

conducted in English. My instructor takes me to Mama
Ngina Road, and pretty soon I'm driving and shifting a car
with a manual transmission on the left side of the road
through traffic.

On my second lesson, I stall the Toyota only once. Goats,
a source of milk and meat, lie on the road to take their afternoon nap. Kenya's version of speed bumps, rectangular
slabs of wood with dozens of spikes pointing up, block a portion of the road, making it a bit like an obstacle course.   I
carefully weave my way through them. They serve their
purpose well, to slow motorists down. Deep potholes filled
with silt and rainwater can swallow half the car. My instructor tells me to drive so close to throngs of roadside pedestrians - within inches - that it scares me. I progress through
several lessons. My curious instructor inquires about US
driving rules. Once I check my blind spot, and he yells,
"Never take your eyes off the road!" I try to explain about
blind spots, and my instructor says, "We don't do that in this
country."

Speaking of women drivers, I notice an article about
women pilots in *The East African Chronicle* of August 4, 1995.
The headline reads "Women better pilots than men," and the
article quotes a study by Britain's Civil Aviation Authority
(CAA) that says men are four times more likely to crash a
plane. It also says:

> "An unpublished study from the Royal Air
> Force's Institute of Aviation Medicine supports
> the CAA. It found that even when the men-
> strual cycle impaired some women, their cock-
> pit skills sank only to the level of men."

Now I'm wondering if I should show this to Jay.

While in Mombasa, I am plagued with headaches, sinus trouble, and cramps and lie down in the afternoon several days while we're here. Mosquitoes love me, and I have several bites on my legs, arms, and face. The heat could be getting to me, too, as there is no air conditioning. It rains at least once a day here, most of the time in the afternoon, and often after dinner as well. Sometimes it rains in the morning, too. The humidity is constant. Often in the afternoon, a rainbow shines over the bay.

I get headaches and earaches often when flying, but they're due to altitude changes and also probably from dehydration. Since there's not an easy toilet solution in the Malibu, I tend to drink less than I should on flights. These ailments are temporary and go away as soon as I land and get something to eat. In Mombasa, something else is going on. It's likely the strain that the place is having on me. I'm very easy-going and don't show what's bothering me, so no one can tell if I'm stressed or not. The contradiction of staying in a Christian mission when I don't believe in witnessing is taking a toll on my health. The fear of not being safe here is a low-level tension that is constant. The physical discomfort is also a factor. All are adding up to the fact that I feel pretty lousy a lot of the time.

I arrange for my mom and dad to send us a care package. My parents function as our stable home team while we are abroad. They retrieve both Jay's and my mail, pay bills that become due, and most importantly, cheer us on with moral support. The last time I traveled around the world, in 1989, their alliance was invaluable. They sent me supplies at key points, encouraged me when I phoned them, and handled daily business at home.

On the phone, Daddy informs me of a certified letter Jay received from his landlord.

"Jay has 60 days to vacate his high-rise apartment," Daddy says. "Apparently they've sold the unit Jay's been renting, and the new owner wants to move in."

I glance at the calendar. We won't even be back in 60 days.

"I'll let Jay know," I tell my dad.

Life back home doesn't stop for us even though we're on our big adventure. The little annoyances continue to happen and have to be dealt with, one way or another. Later, my dad talks to the apartment manager for Jay and arranges an extension.

When the care package arrives, it's filled with travel books, film, some clothes and toiletries, our mail, and some things Jay forgot, including the handheld GPS's battery pack. I arrange to send back a box full of items we no longer need. During our stay, Jay retrieves two parcels from Customs: our newly repaired GPS and a brand new high frequency radio.

Jay is still constantly worrying about the safety of the Malibu. He disconnects the circuit breakers in the airplane so no one can easily start the engine. He removes the newly mended GPS so it won't be stolen by a radio thief. He loses sleep from worrying, and finally becomes physically sick.

We decide to leave Mombasa earlier than originally planned.

9

18 August, 1995
Mombasa, Kenya

"When a flight is proceeding incredibly well, something was forgotten."

—Robert Livingston,
Flying The Aeronca

The people we meet in Mombasa are filled with many dreams. Frank wants to hire an associate to help him run the Center. Roberta wants to improve her surgeries. The workers want to learn computers. The clergy want to convert Muslims. The kids want to ride horses, learn karate, and play. The patients want to see better than before. Jay wants his airplane to be safe. I want to feel better. From this destination, I'm sure there's a lesson I have learned, but I haven't quite sorted it out in my mind. For now, we leave these dreams and pursue our own.

The next round of faxes from Sharon arrives. We have permits and ground handling information for Ethiopia,

Yemen, Oman, India, Pakistan, and Nepal. The original plan was to return to Djibouti, then proceed to Oman. Instead we decide to travel straight to Oman, which will result in a very long flight.

On the last day in Mombasa, Francesca, Roberta's youngest daughter, draws a paper eye for Jay. Thula constructs a paper computer screen for me. Mary, an office worker, writes me a story using the word processor, and Hilton, a computer student, composes a thank-you note. Frank offers me a book on Kenya. I am thrilled with my gift. Jay is bestowed the title of *Mzee*, "respected elder" in Swahili. He receives a nice plaque and a beautiful ebony walking stick, gracious gestures from the staff. Jay is elated.

Kurt, a missionary, drives us to the airport early in the morning in heavy rain. To look official, Jay and I wear our flight uniforms. The plane is full of fuel, one thing Jay took care of on one of his many trips to the airport. We breeze through the formalities and are soon in the air.

Once airborne, the flight path transports us over Kenya, Ethiopia, Djibouti, the Gulf of Aden, and Yemen. Clouds blanket the sky below us, but they don't dampen our mood in the cabin. Jay is tremendously relieved to be leaving Mombasa. The GPS is working again. We test the new high frequency radio, and it is working. The Malibu's air conditioning is still out of service, but it seems like a luxury compared to the GPS and the high frequency radio. Shortly into the flight, we watch the latitude count down to zero on the GPS as we cross the Equator. The engine's hum is strong and steady.

In the air for nine hours, the flight is mostly uneventful. Jay and I take turns flying. Over the Gulf of Aden, the sun sets behind us. We admire a perfect anvil-shaped storm cloud in the distance, lit up by the sunset. During such a long flight, bouts of boredom arise frequently. Boredom is a dangerous enemy in the air that can lead to complacency, or worse, sleep. It has to be actively fought. My favorite way to fight it is to scan the sky for traffic. It's like looking for a tiny silver dot in a huge blue expanse, but I find it challenging and fun. Sometimes the sunlight tricks you and you think there's something there when there's not. When you do find something, you can call it out, as in, "Traffic, three o'clock." You can only see what's ahead and in your peripheral vision, not what's directly behind you. There's no rear view mirror on the airplane. It's up to Air Traffic Control to space aircraft more than a thousand feet apart to avoid in-air collisions.

On this long flight, it's critical that we both stay vigilant, no matter how tired we are. Along the undeveloped Yemeni coast, there is not much light from the ground. The radio crackles but there's little contact. Jay and I start talking to keep each other alert.

"Let's scan the sky for constellations," Jay says wearily.

"Little Dipper," I declare, pointing. With our eyes, we trace the imaginary lines of the Little Dipper.

"Scorpio's tail," Jay says. The stars that comprise the curving tail of Scorpio shine brightly.

Closer to Oman, a British-sounding controller immediately assigns us a squawk code and remains in touch, reporting air traffic commands. We instantly notice the difference in Air Traffic Control service.

Near the end of the flight, we cross the Tropic of Cancer over the northeast tip of Oman.

You'd think there'd be a long line painted on the earth to represent these latitudinal milestones. Only the GPS marks the crossings, however.

As we approach our destination, Muscat, an undercast of

low clouds and the dark night obscure our vision drastically. The haze prevents us from seeing much of anything on the ground. We can't tell whether we're over land or sea. In the mist, we start our descent. We're both worn out. I am weak from not eating for so long.

Close to the ground, the fog finally lifts. Recognizing runway lights, we land. Just after touching down, the engine halts abruptly and the propeller blades freeze. It's horribly quiet. Stopped on an active runway without engine power, we are blocking the way for all airplanes that want to land in Muscat.

The Malibu is almost impossible to start when its engine is hot. Last month in the Azores, the airport crew asked Jay to move the plane from one parking space to another right after we landed. Unable to restart the engine, Jay was forced to return the following morning to move the plane when the engine was cool. A few times in the Caribbean, we've needed to connect the plane to a battery unit to give it a jumpstart. But most places we'll visit this trip will not have the equipment for a small plane such as ours.

Jay musters his energy and tries to shake off his fatigue, adjusts the throttle, opens the mixture to force-flood the engine, makes a determined grimace, and turns the starter. With a lot of cranking, the engine starts roughly, emitting a cloud of smoke. The plane limps onto the taxiway and a marshaller guides us to a parking spot. This flight breaks all previous records: after 12 hours and 41 minutes in the air, I open the door of the plane. The warm, humid ground air feels like I entered a sauna. Jay steps into position for his customary airport picture of the Malibu; he has quite a collection going.

"I can't get a picture," he shouts over at me.

"How come?" I yell back.

"My camera lens is all fogged up," he says, dismayed.

"Won't it clear up in a minute?" I wonder. Usually it's a matter of time.

"Not this time," Jay reports.

An agent from Oman Aviation welcomes us and invites us to board a large, clean, air conditioned bus. Exhausted, Jay and I zombie our way through the modern terminal and then through the special crew lines of Immigration and Customs.

As we exit Customs, we walk down a long roped-off corridor. On the other side, a crowd of roughly a hundred men wearing long white robes and Omani turbans wait for a commercial flight to arrive. The men start to murmur and whisper to each other as we walk past. Sounds of surprise ripple through the entire crowd.

"What are they saying? Is it about me?" I whisper to Jay.

"Don't know," Jay says with a shrug. "Just keep walking."

"We're not holding hands," I say, whispering even more quietly. "Should I be wearing a head cover? Is it my pants?"

I was stumped and Jay wasn't sure. Could it be my uniform with the three stripes on my shoulders? Could it be they've never seen a female pilot before? I'm uncertain about what's causing the whispers, but I am pretty sure it's something about me that's not in agreement with their culture.

At 10:00 p.m., we change money from dollars to Omani *riyal* and eat delicious Indian food at the first airport cafeteria we spot. I stop in the restroom. Each gleaming ceramic toilet comes with an accessorized spray hose. How exciting, my very first spray hose sighting.

One of my hobbies is exploring foreign toilets. Some people visit museums; I visit toilets. Each country displays its own unique personality in its toilets. In parts of Europe, toilets have flat bowls. In Japan, the bowl is in the floor; there's nothing to sit on. In some Italian *pensionnes*, there are two bowls: a bidet accompanies a toilet. Whole books have been written on this subject, such as *Going Abroad, How to Shit in the Woods,* and *Shitting Pretty.*

A taxi takes us one kilometer to the Seeb Novotel, the hotel we pre-arranged with Jeppesen. It's a beauty, with sparkling five-story-high glass windows, pink archways, palm trees, and a manicured lawn. On the hotel door is a sticker labeled Holy Mecca with an arrow and a circle. The arrow tells Muslims which direction to face when they pray. The hotel lobby is expansive, with chandeliers dangling from the ceiling. Uniformed US Air Force men and women stride through the lobby. For the first time in weeks, Jay and I are free of other people's imposed belief systems and can share a hotel room. The water in the shower feels cleaner and safer. The bed feels softer. We're getting along well now that we spent so much time apart in Mombasa and also because we've gotten some of the difficult flying behind us.

Arabs have occupied the land that is currently the Sultanate of Oman since the ninth century BCE. In the seventh century CE, the people converted to Islam and enjoyed a prosperous life. Omani traders spanned the hemisphere from Africa to India. The Portuguese occupied Muscat from 1508 until 1648, when Ottoman Turks took over. Since 1741, the descendants of Sultan Ahmad have ruled the country. Today, Oman is an absolute monarchy and is the fourth fastest growing country in the world. Almost half of its population is under 15 years old. It produces petroleum, copper, fish, fruits, and vegetables. The chief language is Arabic, but English is spoken in business circles.

I read *The Times of Oman*, which is in English, and find interesting local, world, Asian, and African news, sports, and leisure items. Stories from this part of the world are not covered in as much detail in the West, and I relish the rarity.

In the morning, Jay and I dress in casual clothes - long pants - and drive a rented automatic Toyota Corolla all around Muscat and the nearby town of Ruwi. It's cool inside the car, but hot and sunny outside. The roads are sparkling multi-lane masterpieces. Statues and fountains adorn every roundabout. A public park sports gazebos, jungle gyms, and other structures I don't recognize. We drive by His Majesty the Sultan's Palace, his horse stables, his yacht, his 747, the Ministry of This building, the Ministry of That building, and the Ruwi Clock Tower. The buildings are modern and opulent. To go from the broken down infrastructure and poverty in Africa to the blatant excesses of wealth that is Oman in one day leaves us dumbfounded. It's massive culture shock at its best.

Jay's foot is heavy, and the car passes 120 kilometers per hour. A bell sounds, "Ding, ding, ding." It stops when he slows down. There are a few pedestrians in the city center, and Jay shaves one couple a little close. The woman looks straight at us, surprised and indignant.

"Whoa," I say. "Did you just cut it a little close to those people? We're not in Africa anymore, you know."

Jay starts laughing. He realizes he is still driving like he is in Mombasa. He continues to laugh for some time; the culture change really hits his funny bone. We're both in a lighter mood now that we've left the fears and conflicts of Kenya behind. He slows down and drives pedestrian-friendly for the rest of the day.

A shopping mall intrigues us and we stop and park. We walk through a mall that contains a cluster of stores. It doesn't look like a mall does back home; the hallways are designed in somewhat of a maze. I smell pizza and follow the tempting aroma to a Pizza Hut. We devour a vegetarian pizza at this fully automated franchise. The grocery stores are brimming with the best products that both the East and the West have to offer. I notice there are a large number of immigrants here from the Philippines. In a computer store, Microsoft Windows 95 and a 486 computer are prominently displayed. McDonald's offers a veggie burger, a change I would greatly welcome in the US. The local Muscat newspaper is filled with ads for government jobs and contracts to bid on. The houses are huge, and the people look prosperous. If I had previously thought that the United States was the richest country, I'd now have to say I was wrong.

The departure from Oman is smooth, although we do have to wait a bit for avgas. Airport personnel drain fuel from 55-gallon drums into a barrel-shaped container situated on a trailer. The fuel is then hand-pumped into the airplane. Private aircraft and helicopters traveling through Oman require more sophisticated fuel than we do; Oman is just not set up for avgas. Jay orders the fuel in imperial gallons and pays the most expensive price on the entire route, US $5.48 per gallon. Omanis run Jay's crisp $100 bills through a fraud detector.

Our destination today is New Delhi, India. On the way, we'll cross Pakistan, where we have an overflight permit. The cabin is hot, and we are both sweltering. Jay flies the airplane without my help due to the overcast weather. It's IMC (instrument meteorological conditions). Due to our slow climb rate, the air traffic controller instructs us to divert from our planned flight path into Iranian airspace.

Iranian airspace? Yipes, I think. We're not supposed to fly near Iran; we don't hold an overflight permit for that country. The United States and Iran are not exactly on good terms. As a matter of fact, they're not on any terms at all.

Will we be safe?

Jay doesn't seem to have the qualms I do and codes a new waypoint into the GPS. George, the autopilot, turns the plane. Jay calls the Iran air traffic controller to make a position report. What will they say to us? Will we have to go back to Oman and get a clearance? I hold my breath, not knowing what to expect.

"Nice to have you. See you later." Well, that's not exactly what he says, but the Tehran controller's voice is welcoming.

We travel through Iranian airspace without incident and enter Pakistani airspace. Equally friendly, the Karachi controller helps us cut a corner, shaving time off our flight plan. All of the air traffic controllers are helpful and in touch on this flight. I'm pleasantly surprised.

We reach the Indian subcontinent and, between slight patches of thick clouds, glimpse a white salty desert below. It is the Great Rann of Kutch in the state of Gujarat. Over Udaipur and Jaipur, the grassy green fields grow verdant in this monsoon season.

"I don't think I've seen India so lush with vegetation before," Jay says, looking down in amazement. Although he has journeyed to India many times, he's never visited this time of year.

As we approach Delhi, the sky fills with clouds. Jay flies the plane using instruments rather than visual flight rules, where you can simply peer out the windscreen. I search for the runway in this soupy sky. According to the GPS, we're a mere five nautical miles from the field.

Three nautical miles from touchdown and still no sign of the field. Any minute we'll have to abort the landing and perform a go-around procedure called a missed approach if the fog doesn't lift.

Two nautical miles away. Through the haze, I spot two faint lines of lights just ahead.

"Runway lights in sight," I point to the dim outline, almost shouting. There's a tremendous joy during the exact moment you spot the landing strip from the air. It's like winning Bingo and calling it out or finding the final answer to a crossword puzzle, only better. After a long flight in the air, to see the runway is to see an end to the flight and success at hand.

Through the haze that's India, Jay maneuvers the plane into a landing. We park near half a dozen Russian planes and a patch of grass. A car greets us and a man steps out.

"Who is your handling agent?" he says. India does not require us to hire a handling agent who would act as the interface between the pilot and the airport to handle all of the permits, fees, and paperwork, and Jay does not want one.

"We don't have one," says Jay.

"There are three possible agents," says the man. He lists Air India, Indian Air, and a local company. He doesn't act like he is affiliated with any one of them.

Jay shrugs and is hoping to avoid the issue. The man seems to find it strange that we don't have an agent. Maybe everybody does, and we are an exception. In any case, he gives us a ride to the terminal. The man drops us off, and we move on, through Immigration and Customs, forgetting about an agent.

Our regular hotel is full, so we find an alternate. We hire a twenty-something Indian driver to take us to the new hotel. He wears a turban, which only a few Indians do, and this means he is likely a Sikh, a member of a special religion. We climb in the back seat of his white 1950's Hindustan Ambassador sedan, supposedly a step up from a regular taxi. He guns the car and roars through traffic, faster than any other vehicle. The car has no seat belts, no air bags, no head rests, no ABS brakes, no safety equipment at all. At break-neck speed, our driver passes cycles, cars, trucks, cows, motorickshaws, and people, weaving in and out of them. Adrenaline runs fast through my body as it detects our life-threatening situation. Jay and I slide around from side to side in the back seat. By centimeters, the driver misses hitting all sorts of things. The people and animals on the street don't flinch; this is nothing new to them. I glance out the window, then at Jay, then at the driver, knowing that this is bad, but not knowing what to do or say.

"We're not in that much hurry," Jay tries.

The driver speeds up. Does he want a big tip? To keep from sliding completely off the seat, I grab onto a handle. Is he auditioning for stunt man in an American chase scene movie? I'm sure I'll suffer a heart attack, if not a wreck, on the chaotic Delhi streets. I'm starting to sweat; I'm exhausted already from this ordeal. The taxi whizzes by more traffic of all shapes and sorts. Finally, he pulls into the hotel driveway, leaving Jay and me to regain our balance in the back seat one more time.

After we exhale, Jay and I stare at each other in amazement.

"I can't believe we made it," I say.

We know we are taking risks on this trip, but that taxi ride far exceeded our thresholds.

In the morning, at the airport, attempting to leave Delhi is harrowing as well.

23 August, 1995
New Delhi, India

"The knack to flying lies in learning how to throw yourself at the ground and miss."

—Douglas Adams
*Life, the Universe and Everything
(Hitchhiker's Trilogy), p. 73*

*W*ithout a handling agent to grease the wheels of the Delhi airport bureaucracy, Jay and I tackle the labyrinth all by our foreign selves. A 4:00 a.m. start at the airport manager's office leads us to the aviation office in the Domestic Terminal where Jay receives a list of six items to tackle. He hires a cab to the International Terminal and works the list, one by one. My challenging task is to stay put at the Domestic Terminal and watch the luggage.

Hours pass. The temperature in Delhi rises. I read a local English-language paper. An article about cattle on the road catches my eye. It says that during the monsoons, owners let their cattle graze freely without a leash. Although green grass is plentiful, the cows prefer the road, where they forage in the garbage for food. When the cars whiz by, they scare the flies from the cattle, so the cattle like it there. It's not against the law to let your cattle roam freely. The article was about how motorists are losing the race with the cattle in their way.

With the six airport items completed, Jay rides back to the Domestic Terminal, pays fees, and fills out forms. Signatures and carbons are flying now, but we aren't yet. After a cab ride, we and our luggage arrive at Immigration and Customs at the International Terminal to pass the next hurdle. After a shift-change delay, an Immigration officer requests our boarding passes.

"We don't have boarding passes," we explain.

"You can't get through without boarding passes." Several Indian officials confirm each other's decision.

"But we own the plane! Why should we need boarding passes?"

"In Delhi, if you want to leave the airport, you need boarding passes." I can hear the lilt of their Indian accents.

"We have General Declaration forms. Will those do?" we ask hopefully.

The Indian officials nod their heads down, which means yes in America but no in India. "Only boarding passes."

It is all very confusing and frustrating and hot. We are at a standoff. A major international political conflict is brewing right here at the Delhi airport over the absence of boarding passes. I wonder if Amelia had this problem when she flew through India. What will they do with us? Will we be detained and have to stay in India? We wait.

Hours pass. The temperature rises higher.

We locate someone who recognizes a General Declaration form and knows what to do with it. It's a major breakthrough, except for one problem. We don't have a paper imprinted with our time of arrival into the country. To be missing that document is another major political crisis.

We progress to Customs (I don't know how). The man is civilized, thank goodness, or at least he's not as dogmatic about red tape as the others are. He stamps our General Declarations and consents to our departure. I'm happy and excited at this minor victory. Jay and I push a baggage cart filled with luggage about a mile to the airplane, over active taxiways and past uniformed sentries. No one questions us; no one stops us. We load the plane and ditch the cart in the tall grass nearby. Jay climbs in, takes his seat, and straps himself in. I board, secure the cabin door, and take my seat.

Before we can take off, we need to buy fuel, available at the Domestic Terminal. Jay calls to request authorization to start the engine and taxi from the International Terminal to the Domestic Terminal, a one hour trip. Permission granted. With no working air conditioning, in this 40°C (104°F) heat, sweat streams from Jay's face, and I perspire abundantly as we taxi the plane through the maze of runways and taxiways from one terminal to the other.

At the Domestic Terminal, Jay stops the plane in front of a General Aviation hangar. I disembark the plane and run to phone Indian Oil. It will be 30 minutes, they say. At some airports in the US, a pilot can taxi up to a gas pump and fill up, like a car. In most cases, however, an aviator must call a fuel company and wait for a truck to arrive, filled with the correct type of avgas.

We wait. Jay doesn't want to leave the cockpit; he is very anxious to leave Delhi after his administrative nightmares that morning. But the cockpit is approaching oven temperature, and he is forced to step out before he passes out.

In the late morning sunshine, we look for scarce patches

of shade offered by the hangars and offices. A Canadian man approaches Jay. An employee of Pratt & Whitney Canada, he sells airplanes to a startup airline here. He and Jay talk about the airline industry.

A group of men gathers by me and asks, "Where are you from?"

"Dallas, Texas," I say. "We're going all the way around the world," I say with the smallest hint of pride.

"What type of engine does this plane have?"

"A Continental, I believe," I say.

"Is it fuel-injected?" one man asks.

"How much horsepower?" another wonders.

I shrug. Heck, I'm not a mechanic.

"You don't know the engine details of your plane?" the man asks arrogantly.

"I know how to fly it, that's all." Here I was, trying to act like a cool female pilot and it didn't last long.

For the record, here is the engine description: TSIO520BE-1: Teledyne Continental 310-horsepower twin-turbosupercharged intercooled fuel-injected horizontally opposed 520-cubic-inch air-cooled piston engine. We are flying over two oceans in a vehicle with the horsepower of little more than a Nissan Maxima. (17 percent more, to be exact.) Amelia's Lockheed Electra had two engines sporting 350 to 450 horses apiece, depending on what source you want to quote. The female pilots of Amelia's days were definitely engine-maintenance wise. Many of them were terrific mechanics in their own right.

Hours pass. The temperature creeps even higher.

With the help of some employees of India International Airways who let us into their nice air-conditioned office with a phone, we ring the fuel office three or four more times. We can't depart without gas because none is available in

Kathmandu, our next stop. Fed up, Jay marches over to Indian Oil. Their workers have been busy fueling military aircraft all morning.

Around 12:30, the fuel truck shows up. The oil company employees tackle the cabin tank first. Jay climbs in to hold the huge nozzle steady as gas pours into the auxiliary tank. After fifteen minutes, he emerges from the cabin dripping wet and dizzy from the fumes. Workers fill the wing tanks. Jay pays the cheapest price of the whole trip, US $0.87 per gallon. We board. Jay radios the tower so we can get out of India.

The conversation doesn't go well. Our flight plan is cancelled. It's well past the takeoff time window.

The tower employee instructs us to disembark and call the airport office. We do.

The airport official tells Jay he must start all over again with his paperwork.

He's kidding, right?

Wrong. He's serious.

Will we ever be able to leave India? I feel like a captive, with hands, feet, and mouth bound by red tape.

The airport officer notifies Jay that the airport will be closing any minute because the Prime Minister is taxiing and will be taking off soon. But we were here first! (I keep that last thought to myself.)

In a bold move, Jay gently suggests to the airport officer that he could modify the time on the flight plan forms. The airport officer thinks about it and decides, "Gee, I *can* change the time on these documents." So he does, and (put on your party hat) we're cleared for takeoff.

The moment our wheels leave the pavement, airport officials close the Delhi airport to traffic.

I'm not sure why Jay didn't procure an agent. In the briefing book by Donn Kerby, it reads, "Delhi - definitely need agent - probably $300 fee, but worth it and fuel very cheap there; otherwise would be difficult to get from remote parking to offices, etc." Maybe the extra cost soured him on the idea.

In the air, the traffic controllers provide excellent service, and we climb to 11,500 feet in mostly cloudy skies. Monsoonal showers bathe the airplane. For a moment, the clouds part to reveal a lush green valley flooded with swollen rivers. We report our positions at Delhi, Gorakhpur, and Varanasi. From Kathmandu, a rare female voice delivers the air traffic commands.

The sky clouds up fully over Nepal, and the rain starts again, heavier this time. We detour around as many cumulus buildups as we can, but the clouds thicken and the ride becomes bumpy.

Before we left, we asked Nepalese officials if we could land in Bhairahawa, where Jay does volunteer work, instead of Kathmandu. Nepalese officials declined our request to fly the Malibu directly into Bhairahawa since it lacks a Customs staff to receive international arrivals. So we'll fly into Kathmandu and take a commercial flight between Kathmandu and Bhairahawa.

The descent into Kathmandu's Tribhuvan International Airport is one of the most dangerous approaches in the world. Because Kathmandu is located in a valley, the descent must be steep, swift, and perfectly on path, testing the limits of both pilot and airplane. Often the valley is socked in with clouds or fog, as it is today. Jay watches the storms over Kathmandu steadily build on the radar screen.

Sixteen miles from the VOR, we follow the stepped SIERRA approach pattern. At this exact waypoint, the altimeter reads 11,500 feet and mustn't be any lower. In whiteout conditions, rain pelts the windscreen. I always get worried when we fly in the clouds, but I am extra fearful today because I know the mountains are so close by and not visible to us.

I call out the distance checkpoints while Jay monitors the altitude and descends the plane.

"Thirteen," I say. Jay lowers the landing gear and extends the flaps to ten degrees. At thirteen miles we can be no lower than the 10,500-foot level, and we have three miles to reach 9,500 feet.

The rain comes down so hard it shakes the plane. I shiver with trepidation. Jay checks the heading, points the nose down, and heads for 9,500 feet.

"Ten." In two miles, we must drop to 8,200 feet. The plane is heavy with fuel, yet another challenge on this flight. Jay pulls the power back as the plane dives.

In September 1992, Pakistan International Airlines Flight 268 reached the same point where we are right now, only lower. Already at 8,200 feet, they were descending fast. At 9.16 miles out, the Airbus crashed into a 7,300 foot high hillside, obscured by clouds. All 167 passengers and crew died.

"Eight DME," I report. Jay extends the flaps to full and dives the plane for 6,800 feet, an altitude he has two miles to achieve. His fists wrap tight around the yoke as the plane hits a wind gust. He tracks the inbound course of 022 degrees.

In July 1992, the flaps on an Airbus failed to function and were subsequently corrected. But it was too late to perform the approach and the crew asked permission to return to the previous waypoint. Communications between the air traffic controller in Kathmandu and the Thai Airways International crew were muddled and misunderstood. The crew turned right instead of left. A minute later, the GPWS (Ground

Proximity Warning System) announced "Terrain, terrain. *Whoop, whoop.* Pull up." It was too late. The plane crashed into a 16,000 foot peak, killing 113 aboard.

The Malibu is not furnished with a GPWS device. A simple radar altimeter is the closest thing to a GPWS the Malibu contains, but it's utilized during instrument landing approaches and is of limited assistance in terrain avoidance.

Bump. The plane is jostled by the turbulent weather like a toy thrown by a child having a tantrum. We break out of the clouds, and Jay steadies the plane. Only now can we appreciate the emerald hills of the Kathmandu Valley.

At the six mile fix, we descend to 6,100 feet and report the field in sight. For such a bumpy ride, Jay makes a very soft landing on Runway 02, around 4,000 feet above sea level. He takes great pride in his landings and always does an impressive job at making the wheels gently touch the pavement each time.

We park the Malibu at Gate Six. At Gates One through Five sit various Boeings and Airbuses. It's a real sight to see all six planes in a line. The Malibu is significantly dwarfed by the jumbo aircraft. We unload our bags and make our way to Immigration to acquire visas. A Customs official accompanies Jay to the plane and seals it by attaching stickers to the cabin door and luggage compartment that must not be broken until we depart. We ride in a taxi to our favorite lodge, Hotel Garuda in Thamel, where the employees know us and treat us like royalty.

I am madly in love with Kathmandu. On the maze of dusty streets, the Nepali symphony begins. The honks of cars, the clanging bells of bicycle riders, the loud engines of motorcycles, and the murmurs of people dazzle our ear drums. Incense, car exhaust, and cow manure perfume the air. I hate that we only have a week to spend here.

Jay volunteers annually for the Seva Foundation, a group headquartered in Berkeley, California. The word *seva* means "peace" in Sanskrit. The foundation is dedicated to improving the sight of people around the world. Its Nepal office is located in Kathmandu, and the hospital is situated in Bhairahawa, where we'll head next.

The blindness project in Nepal originated in the 1970s. Nepal was the last remaining place on earth where smallpox was still active. Once doctors eradicated the crippling disease, they looked around for another worthy health project and noticed the predominance of blindness from cataracts in this area. Combined with a shortage of ophthalmologists, fighting blindness was a perfect project for the team. A comprehensive study of eye diseases in Nepal was commissioned and published in the 1980s. Among the findings were that roughly nine million bilaterally blind people in India and Nepal could see again if they had access to an ophthalmologist who could perform a cataract-removal operation. Lumbini Rana-Ambika Eye Hospital in Bhairahawa was birthed shortly after the study to meet the eye care needs of Nepal's and northern India's people. Today the project is self-sufficient, even profitable, and the number of ophthalmologists in Nepal has grown.

In the morning, Jay and I split up to run lots of errands. There is no time to be a tourist here due to pressing airplane business and volunteer work. A young, thin motorickshaw driver carries me to the Australian Embassy so I can apply for visas. I am comfortable traveling alone on the streets of Kathmandu, even though I don't know the language and do not look the same as the people here. It's a completely different feeling than what I felt in Mombasa.

Before we left the United States, I was able to obtain almost all the visas we needed, for Djibouti, Kenya, Oman, and India. Nepal demands a visa as well, but you can purchase it at the airport. The same is true for Egypt and the Kiribati Islands. Despite the FedEx shipments and extra rush charges, I lacked one visa before we left: the one for Australia. The only chance I have to procure it is here in Kathmandu. I walk through the gates of the Embassy, then through a lush garden and into what looks like a private mansion. After completing some forms and waiting my turn, I leave the forms and our passports with the Embassy employee.

The motorickshaw driver takes me to the next stop, *Nepal Netra Jyoti Sangh* (National Society of Comprehensive Eye Care). In the business district of Kathmandu, five congested streets come together in an unorganized fashion to make one monster of an intersection. Just off of this intersection in a private complex, the Seva office is housed amid uniform rectangular buildings that look like part of a campus. On the second floor of these brick buildings, I find Jay and Mr. Dhakhwa, the Kathmandu manager, writing a press release for the visit. Mr. Dhakhwa greets me with his bright brown eyes and friendly smile. Spying a computer, I write and fax a quick letter to my parents that lists our revised itinerary.

Jay seeks adventure (yes, more) and wishes to take the local bus to Bhairahawa and return via a commercial airline. Mr. Dhakhwa helps us make return plane reservations from Bhairahawa. After all our errands are finished, Jay and I settle down to a delicious vegetarian dinner of lentils and rice at a restaurant down the street from the hotel. The smells and tastes of the eastern spices of ginger, tamarind, saffron, and curry fill the restaurant and sate our appetite.

In the early morning, Jay is ready to leave for the local bus to Bhairahawa.

"Ready?" he asks me.

"Can I chicken out?" I ask meekly.

"You want to miss out on this adventure of a lifetime?" he jokes with me.

"Sure do. Already got my hands full with as much adventure as I can take. I'm full," I say assuredly.

"OK. See you there," he says.

I buy an airline ticket on Necon Air and call the hospital to ask them if they'll pick me up. Unable to connect to the hospital, I call Mr. Dhakhwa.

"No problem," he says. "Did you see today's *Kathmandu Post*?" he asks eagerly. "There's an article about Jay."

"No. I'll go buy some. Thanks for letting me know!" I say.

I run into the street and buy all the newspaper copies I can find. Back in the lobby hotel, Bim, the hotel desk manager, reads the article with me. It's titled, "Volunteer Eye Surgeon in Nepal," and tells about our flights, Jay's volunteer work, the hospital in Bhairahawa, and the Seva Foundation. I'm thrilled. I feel like a minor celebrity. Bim enthusiastically shows it to all the other people in the hotel's lobby.

In time for my flight to Bhairahawa, I ride a taxi to the airport. The driver is courteous even though the roads are bumpy and the car shows its extreme wear and tear. I advance through the Domestic Terminal, familiar with the plastic seats and the cold concrete floor of the one-room terminal, having waited here many times before. When called in Nepalese, I somehow know which flight is mine and board the small plane. The flight attendant hands out hard candy to eat and cotton to stuff in our ears. From a window seat on the exit row, I notice the door handle is missing. I look over at the other exit door, and it's missing a handle, too. I think about how lucky we are in the United States to have proper safety regulations. I sigh and accept my fate. The engine roars loudly. I look out the window at the valley which forms a lush backdrop for the livestock in this rural country. Halfway through the flight, clouds block my view and I catch up on my reading.

The Kathmandu Post is one of two English papers printed locally. Nepal is a country with lots of issues, and the topics covered in this paper differ a bit from *The Times of Oman*. For example, there is an article on page one about child labor, and one on gender inequality in lending on page three. With all of this moving from culture to culture, I am learning flexibility.

Upon landing at the Bhairahawa airport, Krishna, a driver, and Ganesh, an accountant, greet me. I'm so happy to see faces I recognize from a March visit earlier this year. Both men are fit and stocky and not too tall. They wear white shirts and dark trousers. It's not a uniform, just common dress for men here. Krishna has dark hair and a ruddy complexion from working outside. Ganesh is a fair-complexioned office worker.

Krishna drives us to the hospital and escorts me to Meena's office. She is the chief doctor's assistant. Karn, the controller, Meena, and Ganesh want to learn about our flying adventure. I'd love a status report on the hospital's progress, so for an hour we update each other on these events.

At closing time, Krishna drives me to my favorite hotel, the Yeti. It's right next door to a pig farm, which is muddier than normal due to the monsoons. A sow honks and snorts as I walk into the lobby. The TV in the room changes channels on its own, and the toilet is one of those where there is nowhere to sit. Who could ask for more ambience?

Jay is waiting in the lobby. He can't wait to tell me about his bus trip.

"First, I got on the bus. I waited and waited, but it never

left. It was the wrong bus," Jay explains.

I shake my head.

"Then I boarded this old dilapidated city bus. It took forever to get through Kathmandu's traffic. Outside Kathmandu, we stopped to change a tire. Then we stopped to get petrol. Then we stopped to get lunch. We eventually made it to Butwal," Jay says.

I'm secretly feeling happier and happier I took the plane.

"In Butwal, the bus stopped for many vendors. I've been on and off that bus for ten hours today."

Jay looks tired and thin. However, he seems to flourish on the thrill of the unknown. His threshold is much deeper than mine, I am discovering. This bus trip today, the hiking at Samaria Gorge in Crete, and wanting to go to the beach after two days of heavy sightseeing and travel in Faro are just a couple of examples that make me wonder if I can keep up the pace with Jay. I prefer a familiar, even boring, routine as well as some risk in my life. Will this difference cause problems in our relationship? Time will tell.

The week flies by. Jay performs dozens of eye surgeries. In this country, he can perform a sight-restoring operation in 20 minutes. In one day, he averages about 15 patients. Toward the end of the week, Jay delivers a lecture on refraction to the staff. At night, he sniffles and snorts like he is developing a cold.

I meet with Mr. Karn to review the hospital's new accounting system. In March, he and I installed Intuit's Quicken accounting program and began entering the hospital accounts. For three months, Karn compared the computer's results with his paper ledgers. He forwarded the reports to the auditors, and they authorized him to start using Quicken. On the first of July, he turned the system on. The change saves him two hours a day that he will use analyzing accounts or studying patient trends. I am thrilled that he's made so many steps forward on the project since March. Mr. Karn hands me a gift, a Sanskrit calendar for the year 2052, Nepal's current year. I am delighted.

In March, I also installed a copy of Borland's Paradox database. Dr. Dhital, Karn, Ganesh, and I designed a database to store information about the patients. The staff hoped to investigate diseases by geographical area to determine where preventive education could be most effective. For example, a disease called xerophthalmia, a Vitamin A deficiency that causes blindness and usually occurs in young boys, can be prevented with parent education. It's a cultural and educational issue: boys, revered in the Nepali and Indian culture, are fed only meats when they are young. A healthy diet necessitates green leafy vegetables to provide essential Vitamin A. To thwart blindness from xerophthalmia, the hospital staff can instruct mothers in affected areas to feed their boys more leafy veggies. The database can show the staff where to concentrate their training efforts.

I can appreciate how rewarding it must be for Jay to help people regain their vision. How many people do you know who can make blind people see, literally? Participating in the database project, I feel proud to be a small part of this phenomenal operation.

I depart for Kathmandu a day earlier than Jay to wrap up our business at the Australian Embassy and to start on the Nepali departure paperwork. It's pouring rain when my plane lands, and my clothes and I become completely soaked simply walking from the plane to the terminal. The following day, the last day of our planned time in Kathmandu, I call Jay in Bhairahawa.

"I haven't gotten any faxes from Sharon," I say. "Plus I haven't been to the Embassy, but I'm going as soon as I hang up with you."

"Hmm. We might have to stay another day in Kathmandu then," Jay deduces. "We can't go without the permits."

"OK. I'll see you tonight when you get here."

The same motorickshaw driver as I had last week drops me at the Australian Embassy about thirty minutes before they close. It's near rush hour, and the driver's bicycle bell *"ring-rings"* more often as a warning for the other traffic. I retrieve our passports and visas with no time to spare. I visit Kathmandu's aviation office and am notified that all our forms are in order. Our permit faxes appear from Jeppesen at 5:00 p.m. They are for India, Myanmar, and Malaysian overflights and Thailand and Indonesia landings. Everything pulls together at the last minute. We have all the documents we need to leave Kathmandu after all. It's too late to call Jay; he's probably at the Bhairahawa airport or on his way back to Kathmandu already.

Jay arrives in Kathmandu on Nepal Airways and asks the crew to assist him with a low tire on the Malibu. A maintenance worker injects nitrogen in the tire and tightens a belt, all at no cost. The Nepalis are glad to lend a hand.

Jay walks into the hotel, fully expecting to stay another night.

"All the paperwork is here. We can leave tomorrow as planned," I tell him, smiling.

"Great," Jay replies.

Later that night, my father phones the Hotel Garuda at our weekly, pre-arranged time.

"Your mother is in the hospital," he says, his voice slow but steady.

"What for?" I say lightly, hoping it's something minor.

"She's had a stroke," Daddy says.

11

29 August, 1995
Kathmandu, Nepal

"I was always afraid of dying. Always. It was my fear that made me learn everything I could about my airplane and my emergency equipment, and kept me flying respectful of my machine and always alert in the cockpit."

—*General Chuck Yeager,*
Yeager, An Autobiography

"*I* found your mother slumped over on the floor near the couch," Daddy continues.

I'm unable to speak. I visualize the white couch in the living room of their big home. I can't quite picture Mama on the floor, just lying there.

"She's doing fine and has been moved to rehabilitation already," Daddy says reassuringly. He is trying to cushion the shock of the news. "She's lost some movement in her

right side, but the therapists say she could recover completely."

"How long has she been in the hospital?" I ask, trying to
regain my composure.

"She had the stroke on the 24th. I took her to Emergency
then."

That was five days ago. For five days, I was unaware my
mom was lying in a hospital bed. I'm numb; my emotions
are frozen. Why didn't Daddy call me earlier? I feel helpless
and very far away from my family. Nepal is on the exact
opposite side of the earth from my home, 12 time zones
away. When it's 10:00 p.m. here, it's 9:45 in the morning at
home. I want to reach out to them, but I don't know how to.

"I should come home…"

Daddy interrupts. "We discussed that. Your mother
wants you to continue your trip and not worry about her
until you get home."

"How can I possibly not worry?" I ask, not really expecting an answer.

"She has a great medical team looking after her at
Medical City. A neurologist, a speech therapist, and a physical therapist are all working to help her recover. She's lost a
bit of movement in her leg, arm, and face, but she's gaining
a little back every day."

"I know you've arranged the best care for her. Can I talk
to her?" I ask.

"Maybe later," Daddy says.

I switch my thoughts from Mom to Dad. "Are *you* OK?"

"I'm doing fine," Daddy says. "You know me. I'm a survivor."

My dad has been through quite a life. From surviving
Word War II to managing several family hardships, he is definitely a survivor in the grandest of terms.

"OK. I'll call tomorrow when we get to Thailand. We're leaving first thing in the morning," I tell him. I can't do anything tonight.

There is really nothing else I can do except worry and cry, and I don't want to do either of them on the phone. Jay overhears the conversation and is greatly concerned. He is helpful and explains that it might be related to my mom's diabetic condition. I sleep intermittently and restlessly. I lie awake thinking about whether I should go home anyway, even if Mama says she doesn't want me to stop the trip. As a daughter and the only living child in my family, I should be by my Mom's side. Life doesn't stop for us even though we're on our big adventure.

In the morning, we reach the airport at 6:15. We can pack away our uniforms for the rest of the trip and relax in our tourist-wear. Jay files the flight plan and receives a weather report. There are typhoons in Korea, Vietnam, and the Indonesia area. I navigate through Immigration, Customs, and airport security.

At the plane, Jay pours in a fresh quart of oil. With no officials around, Jay breaks the Customs seals, and we climb in. We take off on the ECHO 2 departure route to partly cloudy skies and hills all around, climbing as fast as we can, considering the hot cylinder head temperature that we always have to watch. I try hard to focus on the flight and not Mama's stroke, but it isn't easy.

From Kathmandu, we travel over India, talking to Calcutta control. We skirt a corner of Bangladesh airspace. Calcutta control hands us over to Dhaka control.

"November-Three-One-Three-Juliet-Mike, Dhaka control," an air traffic controller grumbles in a Bangla accent.

"Dhaka control, Three-Juliet-Mike, go ahead," Jay replies.

"Three-Juliet-Mike, Dhaka control, what is your overflight permit number?"

Jay pauses. We have permits for India, Myanmar, Malaysia, Thailand, and Indonesia, but not Bangladesh. The chart says it's not necessary at the flight level we're at, 15,000 feet.

"Dhaka control, Three-Juliet-Mike, we do not have a permit for Bangladesh," Jay says.

"Three-Juliet-Mike, Dhaka control, you must have a permit. In order to fly in our air space, a permit is required. What is your permit number?" Dhaka control repeats himself.

"Dhaka control, Three-Juliet-Mike, flight level 150, understand no permit required," Jay says.

"Three-Juliet-Mike, Dhaka control, you must have a permit. Do you not have a permit?"

"Dhaka control, Three-Juliet-Mike, we do not have a permit," Jay is now repeating himself.

What is it with paperwork in this part of the world? I am perturbed, even though I probably should be a little more concerned.

"Three-Juliet-Mike, Dhaka control, relay your operator name, address, and takeoff weight," the controller says gruffly.

Cautiously, Jay gives him the answers over the airwaves so the controller can fill out his form.

The controller continues to make a big stink about our not having a permit. Jay looks at the GPS to see how many minutes we have left in Bangladeshi airspace. Any fear I have of breeching Bangladeshi airspace dissipates the more the controller argues with Jay. It reminds me of the challenge we had leaving Delhi.

"Twenty minutes left," Jay reports. Jokingly, he speculates, "Do you think their MiGs can intercept us before we leave Bangladeshi airspace?"

"No way," I joke back. "They'd have to fill out a bunch of paperwork first."

Below, the azure Bay of Bengal meets the Mouth of the Ganges south of Bangladesh in a muddy mix of blue and brown waters. Clouds blanket Myanmar, selfishly hiding the scenery of this mysterious land. An airline pilot calls Yangon air traffic control. No answer. Several more aviators try with the same result. "Maybe it's tea time," one of the pilots says jokingly.

Over Thailand, between billowy buildups, a beautiful forested valley lies below. We contact a Bangkok controller, who turns us over to Chiang Mai approach. Jay descends the plane and lands according to the controller's instructions. He stops in front of the tower. The modern multi-story airport building looks brand new and very impressive.

An airport employee escorts Jay and me into the building and through a VIP line. Afterwards, the employee ushers us to a desk where two ladies hand us many forms to fill out. Their Thai-accented English is slow and understandable. One lady guides us to Customs and Immigration. We change money and book a hotel, the Chiang Mai Plaza. I fax Daddy to give him the hotel phone number.

Jay's sniffles and snorts from Bhairahawa turn into a full-blown cold. He stays in the room and takes a bath while I explore the streets of Chiang Mai. I pick up a few tourist brochures to see what the main attractions might be. I pass by a healthy-looking vegetarian restaurant and make note of it for later. I love walking around in grocery stores and markets to survey the local foods. Each time, the fish, the fruits, and the vegetables are different from what is available at home. I can try something new, like the bright red rambutan fruit, which tastes sweet and exotic. I admire the colorful artistry of the vendors in the market, silvery glistening fish arranged in circles, tail in teeth.

Back at the hotel I call Daddy to see how Mama is doing. Because of the time zone differences in this part of the world, I can only call early in the morning or late at night. At 8:30 p.m. in Thailand, it's 8:30 a.m. in Dallas.

"She is the same," he says. "She's coherent and slowly improving, working on regaining the feeling in her leg, arm, and face."

"Can I talk to her?" I ask.

"Not yet, but soon," Daddy says. I wonder if he's telling me everything about her condition.

In the morning, it is raining from tropical storm "Lois," coincidently my mother's name. The *Bangkok Post* carries the headline, "North, Northeast reel under fury of Depression Lois." A picture shows a man in a blue shirt holding an umbrella and standing waist-high in water next to a sub-merged Shell gas pump in Chiang Mai's Doi Saket District. I read the rest of the paper and am struck by an article on two gibbons named George Bush (Sr.) and Saddam Hussein. At only a few months old, they were illegally smuggled to the Philippines and have now been returned. The gibbons' han-dlers say that they were "rather naughty while they were in the Philippines" and that "Saddam is a little wild, but Bush is obedient." After reading this article, I'm convinced that the rest of the world has more fun than the serious United States. Perhaps it's time to lighten up. Thais have a word in their language, "*sanuk*." It means fun, pleasurable, and enjoyable.

Jay is feeling a bit better, and a tour occupies our after-noon. We visit Meo Village and Doi Suthep Temple. At the Meo Village, we see the Meo hill tribe who dress in colorful traditional robes and headgear and live in the lush forested jungle valleys of Doi Sutheo Mountain. The guide discusses the life of a tribesman and shows us a museum which contains poppy plants and the femur of an elephant. We take a tram to Wat Prathat Doi Suthep Temple, which is 3,500 feet above sea level. Legend has it that a white elephant stood at the site where the temple is now, trumpeted loudly, circled three times, and kneeled. That's how they knew it was an auspicious site where they should build a temple. The temple is high enough to offer a panoramic view of the city, but today it is socked in with clouds and fog. At the temple, we remove our shoes in deference to the Thai culture.

Thais have many beliefs that should be followed when in their country. The head is the most sacred part of the body, so the worst thing that a foreigner can do is to touch another's head. You'd never pat them on the head, even if you have friendly intentions. The feet are special, too, and Thais do their best to hide them, since this is the lowest part of the body. Never use your feet to point, especially in a temple. Cover your legs and shoulders while entering a temple, and never climb on a Buddha image. Instead of a handshake, the greeting is to hold the palms of your hands together below your chin, very similar to the Christian prayer position. In India, this means, "I salute the God in you." I'm not sure if Thais interpret it the same way. Emotional outbursts as well as signs of affection are to be avoided in public. The Thais deeply respect their Royal Family, so it's better not to say anything bad about them, even if it's a joke. Thais also revere personal hygiene and cleanliness.

Now that I've said all this, let me also explain that Thais are mostly Buddhists, and Buddhists are pretty much fine with anything you do. Another phrase, "*mai pen rai,*" means "never mind." However, if you do follow customs, you'll be highly esteemed.

Thoughts about my mom fill my head during the tour. If I can't be in Dallas to support her, what can I do from here? As soon as I get back, I call my friend and ex-husband Ernie to ask him to see if he can help my dad. I call my favorite florist and send Mama a get-well bouquet of flowers. I write and send a fax to her.

> To: Mom
> From: Sandi
> Subject: Get Well
> Hi Mom,
> By the time I can get a card to reach you by mail, it will be forever, so I am sending this fax instead. Pretend it's a get well card!
> I wish I could be there now, but I can't come up with an easy answer. You're in good hands with therapists and doctors so if you follow their advice and work hard, you will be recovered in no time. Jay says that if you had a diabetes-related stroke, most (a very high percentage) people recover fully.
> I'll be thinking good thoughts about you and hope we can talk soon. We are finally back in the more civilized countries for a while. There is a tropical storm named after you: "Lois." It's near Vietnam which caused some rain here today! The weather is very mild here compared to Dallas weather - Dallas is among the most severe in the world.
> I miss you and I'll just try to get back as soon as I can. At least we have already accelerated the schedule to get home earlier than October. Hang in there and get well!
> Love,
> Sandi

The next morning, I am sniffling and snorting. Perhaps I am catching Jay's cold. We consume the bountiful buffet breakfast at the hotel, which includes fancily carved pineapple, melon, and local fruits. We shop for a walking stick that Jay wants and sightsee at temples and burial places. It is quite hot and I do not feel well, so I walk back to the hotel to lie down and rest. In the evening, Daddy calls.

"Your mother is experiencing a severe pain in her stomach. The doctors don't know what it is and are going to perform exploratory surgery on her," Daddy explains.

"Oh, no," is all I can say.

"This is serious, Sandi. More so than the stroke."

"It sounds serious, especially since the doctors don't know what's causing the pain." I can barely get the words out.

"The doctors are not hopeful," Daddy says grimly. He always breaks things to me gently, slowly. "Nothing showed up on the tests they ran."

"I wish I could be there right now," I tell him.

"I'll call when she is out of surgery," Daddy says.

"OK."

I call ICU several more times. The doctors perform a colostomy on my mother, making a hole in the side of her belly. Jay gets on the line to help me understand what a colostomy is. A colostomy causes the digestive system to be rerouted as a portion of the lower intestines are removed. Mama's outlook is grim. I'm bordering on hysterics.

Jay explains how strokes can create blood clots from the heart that can travel to other parts of the body. Apparently there is a blood clot in her stomach causing the pain and trouble. Jay is helpful and patient explaining the medical terms of my mother's illness.

I'm upset, afraid, and irritated that I am stuck here in

Thailand and not by my mother's side where I should be. The guilt is weighing heavily on me.

"Jay, I think I should go home," I say.

Jay becomes noticeably upset at my comment. "I can't finish the trip without you. I'll be stuck here," he says nervously.

Jay's lack of support takes me by surprise. To me, he seems to be thinking only of himself. "Don't you think family is more important than some silly risky adventure?"

"No," he replies.

"Wow." Stunned, I don't understand his point of view.

"If you leave, I don't think you'll come back," he admits.

"Of course I would come back in just a couple of days." He has a point though. My mom's illness is not a short-term event.

Full of emotion, I can't see clearly what to do. Jay is tired and cranky and doesn't want to talk any more. I feel that this is a pretty big difference in our value systems. At 1:00 a.m., with no resolution on this issue, I go to bed but I do not sleep.

12

2 September, 1995
Chiang Mai, Thailand

"You'll be bothered from time to time by storms, fog, snow. When you are, think of those who went through it before you, and say to yourself, 'What they could do, I can do.'"

—*Antoine de Saint Exupéry,*
Wind, Sand, and Stars, 1939.

*I*n the morning, we take a taxi to the airport, pay the fees, clear Customs and Immigration, and walk out to the plane. I load the luggage while Jay files the flight plan to Singapore and obtains a weather report.

The flight is easy with no auxiliary fuel tank and no high frequency radio to deal with. We climb fast to 15,000 feet without a hint of overheating in the cylinder head temperature. Thin clouds with rain just above freezing accompany us for most of the flight. The Seletar approach controller asks

Jay to circle the field, then land. The Seletar Airport is a small local airport north of the city center. It makes sense to avoid the large international airport when a smaller one is available that is more equipped to handle General Aviation needs.

Jay and I are now old pros at ground handling. We sail through Immigration and Customs with our General Declaration forms, and move on to the airport office to complete more forms. We look for a reasonably priced hotel, and a local man helps us call a taxi. Thirty minutes later, a taxi arrives to whisk us off to the York Hotel. When he speeds, the car makes a sound, "*ding, ding,*" just like the rent car in Oman.

It's easy to walk all around Singapore. The streets are clean, and the city is more modern in some ways than US cities. Tolls are automated in and out of the city. Fast food restaurants abound in the form of food courts, offering every style of food you can dream of. Citizens are peculiarly compliant about the laws here, even traffic laws. If a crosswalk light says "don't walk," no one dares to walk until it says walk. It doesn't matter if there are no cars for miles. Everyone stays perched on the edge of the curb but not an inch over.

For dinner, we treat ourselves to the fare at a vegetarian restaurant. The restaurant owners offer a very pure way of living: there is no meat, no smoking, no alcohol, and no bottled drinks on the menu. I have my fill of *pulao, chapatis,* lentils, and other Indian cooking. After dinner, the streets are filled with people. It's far safer here than in Dallas. But it's oppressive here too; I feel like I could be arrested any minute for breaking a law I'm not aware of.

Amelia landed in Singapore on June 20, 1937 and promptly collected a $25 prize for winning a race with a KLM plane from Rangoon. Her equipment was holding out well; she suffered only a broken fuel analyzer, and KLM promised to help her with repairs on her next stop in Indonesia. She did not stop to sightsee in any of the places she landed, with one exception. In Karachi, Pakistan, she took two camel rides because she thought it would spice up her story-writing for the press. Heat was a factor for her throughout the trip. Traveling so close to the Equator, temperatures were oppressive and, with no air conditioning, she had no relief from the heat, even at night.

At the hotel, Jay calls his mom and dad and a couple of friends to give them an update on our trip. I talk to Daddy. Aunt Kid, my dad's sister-in-law, has flown in from Philadelphia. Kid is a nickname that my aunt has always had since I've known her; her real name is Mary. At first, it scares me to hear that Kid flew down. It makes it that much more serious for me. Yet, I'm very happy that Daddy has someone to go through this with. Kid and Daddy are close; Daddy lived with his brother Francis and Kid after World War II. Later Kid and Daddy worked together in my dad's business. With Kid by his side, this takes a little bit of the pressure off of me to go home immediately.

"Mom is stable," Daddy says. "She has a tube in her mouth from the surgery. She cannot talk."

Kid chimes in. "But she has communicated. She wrote the words 'glasses' and 'TV' on a piece of paper. So we gave them to her. It was great to see she was feeling well enough to ask for them."

"That is great news," I say. "Is she still in ICU?"

"Yes. She's going to need more time in ICU. We're not out of the woods yet," my dad says. Wishing I could somehow do more that would make a difference, I settle for sending Mama a fax on York Hotel stationery.

In the morning, Jay and I wear shorts in the hot, sunny

weather and travel around Singapore using the MRT (Mass Rapid Transit). It's a clean, efficient light rail system that is environmentally-friendly and which covers the downtown area.   We start at the Orchard station, ride with local Singaporeans, and disembark at Raffles Place. In Singapore, many places and buildings carry the name of Sir Thomas Stamford Raffles who established the British colony in Singapore. He also spent time in Indonesia and wrote a two-volume history of Java. By the Singapore River, Jay and I spot a statue of Raffles at the place where he supposedly landed in 1819.

We spy the Merlion statue in our walk by the river. It has the head of a lion and the body of a fish and is riding on a crest of waves. The statue is all white, is nearly nine meters high, and weighs 70 tons. The lion's mouth spurts water into the harbor. The Merlion is a protected symbol of Singapore Tourism. Singapore gets its name from the Sanskrit word *singapura*, which means lion (*singa*) and city (*pura*). The legend states that an 11th century prince named the city after seeing a lion.   The Merlion is the symbol for the ancient city of Temasek, which is Javanese for the sea, and which stood in the same location as Singapore before Temasek was destroyed in the fourth century CE.

We spot a Chili's restaurant and can't resist going in and having an American meal for a change. For the first time in two months, I eat a salad since the water here is safe to drink. My talk about leaving for home has Jay on edge. He is polite but distant during the activities we do together. I feel emotionally drained and abandoned.

After sightseeing, we ride the MRT back to the hotel. In *The Sunday Times*, I find numerous places where people are praised for good behavior and, in some cases, rewarded by the government. A page full of graduation announcements congratulates good students on their milestone. One hundred courteous drivers were pulled over and given a plaque, a certificate, and two Shell vouchers worth Singapore $80.00. Pass a fitness test and you'll receive $30.00 off the yearly insurance premium. I see an article on reducing the excesses of state welfare, citing Belgium's and Holland's changes to cut income support if recipients refuse to accept training, do not seek work, or turn down a job. An announcement heralds Singapore's first Internet café. These articles are so different from what I might find in the Dallas paper that I am intrigued. I pay the hotel bill to save time in the morning.

The next day, the wake-up call doesn't come. The phone is cut off since I paid the bill already. I also can't call for a taxi from the room. Sometimes Singapore can be a little too efficient for its own good.

In spite of the absent wake-up call and taxi hassles, we leave Singapore for Bali, Indonesia at a reasonable time. Jay has me do a lot of the flying. Perhaps it's his way of trying to get my mind off my mom. Most of the way, the flight is clear and beautiful. I wear long pants because we will be entering a Muslim country. As we approach the islands, clouds appear again. Mount Bromo's black volcanic landscape towers above the clouds in the sky as we fly by. Air traffic controllers issue us vectors for the approach to Bali's airport. Jay makes a right downwind turn and lands. Bright sunshine and hot temperatures greet us on the ground.

We decide to buy fuel now since it's still early in the day. Employees of the fuel company fill the wing tanks. We won't need to fill the auxiliary tank until we start over the Pacific Ocean. The hot Indonesian sun reddens my face. A Customs officer greets us at the plane. Inside the airport office, we complete some forms and move through Immigration. From there we find a hotel booking desk. The lady at the desk recommends the Sheraton Nusa Dua, so we take a taxi there.

I finally bring the subject up. "Well, if I don't go back to Texas, what can we do to get me home sooner?" I'm hoping Jay has a perfect solution, but I know he won't.

He doesn't say anything.

"Can we leave here a day earlier than planned?" I ask.

Jay agrees reluctantly.

We're just not in the same place emotionally right now. Jay's spirits continue to soar as the flights progress successfully. After all, we're doing the dream of his lifetime. My spirits have sunk to new lows with my mother in the hospital. It's a tough predicament for both of us. I don't want to mess up Jay's dream, but I want to be home for my mother. It is a shame to miss out on the benefits of paradise, but I can hardly enjoy sightseeing with all the guilt I am feeling about not being by my sick mother's side. If something happened to her, I know I would be full of regrets about what I did and didn't do. We check in for two nights instead of three.

At the Sheraton, a gentleman hands us each a welcome drink. We walk past a pool, fountains, a waterfall, and a cave. The grounds are lusciously landscaped with tropical plants and flowers. Our room is a nicely-furnished suite overlooking the beach. The toilet has its own closet. The shower has enough room that you can sit down. Next door, there is a real lagoon with lilipads floating on top and ducks swimming around in the water. The waves crash rhythmically into the sand yards from our room. Birds sing and chirp contentedly. Wow, what an unbelievable hotel, I think. I feel even more torn.

At night, Jay and I attend a dinner dance show. It's the first time we splurge and enjoy evening entertainment on the trip. The dance is the Ramayana Ballet, a classical dance drama that acts out a Hindu story about a prince named

Rama and his wife Sinta. Sinta is kidnapped by another king on the way to a forest. An eagle tries to save her, but is defeated. Rama leads a troop of monkeys to save Sinta and they are reunited. The dancers are graceful, and their costumes are elaborate. The stage is bright with the colors of the set, costumes, and makeup of the dancers. After the dance, a trio of Sumatrans serenades us with Mexican songs. Jay gets such a kick out of this that he sings along loudly.

> *"One guantanamera*
> *Guajira, one guantanamera*
> *One guantanamera*
> *Guajira, one guantanamera*
>
> *Yo soy un hombre sincero*
> *De donde crecen las palmas..."*

After dinner, I call Daddy and Kid to see how Mama is doing.

"The tube in her mouth has been removed," Daddy reports.

"Can I talk with her?" I ask again.

"Not today," he says.

It's frustrating not to be able to hear Mom's voice and, especially, not to be there. Kid gets on the line and chats with me some more about how my dad is holding up. I'm so glad that she is there with him. It has to be unbearable for him. They have been married 45 years. I send Mom a fax on Sheraton Nusa Dua stationery, trying to do what I can from where I am.

> Hi Mom!
> I hope you're feeling better. Pretty soon you'll
> be out of ICU and in a regular hospital bed - maybe

already. Doctors say you're doing well.

I am slowly making my way east. Yesterday we flew from Singapore to Indonesia. We are staying at a touristy hotel in Bali, not our style usually but other hotels were full. Still have to avoid salads and tap water. Since leaving the US, I have only had Singapore tap water - have bought bottled water and even use it to brush my teeth. I haven't been sick.

Hope to see you soon. I may fly back from Darwin, Australia, the next stop, for a very short time.

Get well!

Love,

Sandi

The following day, Jay hits the beach. It's hot and humid in this tropical country, and I decide to go shopping instead. You're expected to bargain with the vendors on prices except at the department stores and shopping centers. In the afternoon, we reunite for a tour of the Bali countryside and the local attractions. Bali is only one of over 13,600 islands in the Republic of Indonesia, which is the fourth most populated country in the world.

First, we stop at a rice field where workers burn the plants to keep insects off them. The workers also beat the dried plants. Rice is a major staple of the Indonesian diet. Our guide, Darpata, tells us that Indonesians have many words for rice, more than what can be translated into English.

The tour transports us to a compound where an extended family lives together. I query Darpata on whether I should take my shoes off in the house. Darpata smiles and replies, "I'll never tell you if you are wrong." Hmmm. What does that mean? It must be the polite culture they have here. If you are doing something you shouldn't, a local person will ask you, "Where are you from?" or "Where are you going?" but they won't tell you what you're doing wrong. You must subtly pick up the clue. Unfortunately, nothing about me is subtle. I still don't know whether I should remove my shoes.

Ninety percent of Balinese practice Bali-Hinduism, a religion that's older than 3,000 years. They believe in spirits and animism and offer fruits and flowers to appease angry deities. We visit a monkey forest called Alas Kedaton. This place is considered holy and the monkeys are sacred. The monkeys live in this natural habitat far above ground in tall nutmeg trees and have been fed repeatedly by tourists. Jay, always testing his limits, attracts one's attention and is nearly bitten. Fruit bats sleep hanging in the trees as well.

Next, we motor to Tanah Lot, a beautiful temple situated on a striking cliff at the edge of the sea. At sunset, our cameras snap the Kodak-moment photo when the temple appears in silhouette.

At the very end of the tour, Jay shows Darpata a photo of the airplane and explains about our trip around the world. It sinks in slowly for Darpata that Jay owns the plane and doesn't just have a special commercial ticket. He gasps when he realizes it.

"You are my first client like that," he sputters and laughs. What a face he projects. "I think you are the richest man in Indonesia." It must be the culture, where it is so hard for Darpata to fathom that it is possible to own a plane without being really wealthy.

In this comfortable paradise, I sleep late. All of 15 minutes. Up at 5:45 a.m., it is time to fly to Darwin, Australia. Jay can't find his wide-brimmed hat, so he dons a cap with the Malibu logo on it. We both wear shorts to try to stay cool in this weather.

In clear skies, we take off in a mild headwind and climb to 15,500 feet. Cloud-covered islands, towering mountaintops, and a blue-on-blue horizon infuse the morning scene. The engine buzzes along. We pass Lombock and Timor. The air traffic controllers gain an Aussie accent. Our descent into Darwin, Australia is normal.

Darwin was a critical stop for Amelia. By June 28, 1937, the day she landed in Darwin, her husband was pressuring her to be home by the fourth of July. She had flown over 20,000 miles in over 140 hours of flight time. She had flown 20 out of the 27 days of the trip with way too little crew rest time. In preparation for her flight to Howland, the Navy asked her for radio frequency details, not a strength of Amelia's. Because there were so many people involved, the Navy received several different answers. Amelia had more than three strikes against her: flight coordination with the Navy was missing, her radio training and mastery were substandard, fatigue was clouding her judgment (although one could make a case that she was so much of a risk-taker, she never really had prudent judgment), Amelia's navigator was drinking, and Howland Island was such a tiny speck that it would take a miracle of navigation to find it with the tools available in 1937. A fatal disaster was inevitable.

When Jay and I land in Darwin, airport employees instruct us to taxi to the Customs area and remain inside the plane. A quarantine officer walks up to our plane and hands Jay a spray can through a tiny cockpit opening.

"Spray the inside of the plane with this can," the quarantine officer says. "Do not open your doors until I return," he adds. Then he walks away.

"We can't get out?" I shriek. "I don't want to be deloused." I am full-out whining now.

"They're not going to give us anything that will kill us," Jay says, always looking at the ultimate consequences. He starts spraying with the can of what looks like insecticide. I turn my head.

"Ugh." I squench up my face. I breathe shallowly as best I can, not knowing what the stuff is. The hiss of the can gives way to a perfumed smell. Why do they try to make insecticide smell good, I wonder silently? Minutes later, another Customs officer says to open the door of the plane. We climb out of the cabin, and I take a deep breath of fresh air, coughing for effect. The officer has us complete several forms and stamps our passports. Before we reposition the plane from the Customs parking space to General Aviation, we peek inside the terminal. Jay picks up some brochures and a Diet Coke. I locate a tourist desk and choose a hotel. Stealthily, I check into air tickets back to Texas. It is 4:53 p.m. local time, and offices are about to close. A travel agent at the airport desk is willing to work on an itinerary for me. I know better than to bring it up with Jay.

Back at the airplane, we taxi to General Aviation and park in front of Phoenix Aviation. Jay asks a mechanic there about changing the Malibu's oil, performing a maintenance check, and inspecting the broken air conditioning. He confirms that he can do the work. He meets a helicopter pilot, who graciously calls a taxi for us from his mobile phone.

At the Value Inn, the desk clerk, a pilot who flies a four-seat Cessna 172, spies Jay's Malibu cap. "Do you have a Malibu?" he asks as he checks us in.

"Yes, and we've flown it three quarters of the way around the world so far," Jay replies.

The desk clerk's eyes get real big, and he inquires about the plane and our flight.

Jay gives him all the details. That conversation puts Jay

in a good mood. I ring the travel agent, who informs me the price for the ticket from Darwin to Dallas is Australian $6,000.00 (a little over US $4,000). That's a lot of money for me. I thank her, not ready to commit to anything.

We settle into the hotel room, which is one-fourth the size of any we have had on the trip. This tiny cube is built as compact as it can be, with the bed taking up most of the room. The bathroom door bumps up against the bed. A toilet, shower, and sink are crammed into the square bathroom. There is no phone or coffee maker in the room. No luggage storage or wake up call service is available. You have to pay in advance. I think they're taking this "value" part of Value Inn seriously by offering a truly no-frills hotel.

Jay is starving and we walk to a Thai restaurant and eat dinner there. On the way, Jay loquaciously comments about the flight we just finished, what he wants to see here, and the right-hand drive cars, some dating to the 1950s and 1960s, that we see on the way to the restaurant. He is normally fairly talkative, but tonight he is more so. I think he's relieved we've made it to Darwin, where we can get service for the Malibu. I think he's also trying to take my mind off my Mom's dilemma and help me enjoy the rest of the trip.

Later that evening, I call Daddy and Kid to see how Mama is doing. I hate having to wait all day before I can call. I can still only call first thing in the morning or last thing at night because of the time zones. Mama is still in ICU. She still can't talk.

I'm not sure what to do. My choices are miserable. Should I abandon Jay and abort the mission? He could find someone else to take my place. Or could he? Should I delay the trip and fly back, only to have to turn around, abandon my mother, and come back? Her illness will require a very long recovery time. I can't delay the trip until she is fully recovered. Should I stay here with Jay, leaving my family alone to fend for themselves? I'm in agony over this.

None of these alternatives is acceptable to me, but I'm determined to make the decision that will work best for all of us: my family, Jay, and me. Maybe I can convince Jay to compromise and accelerate the schedule. We could finish the trip, and I could arrive home as early as possible. I would also be home permanently and wouldn't have to leave after only a couple of days. It seems the most desirable option at the moment - if I can talk Jay into it.

7 September, 1995
Darwin, Australia

"It is not easy to be the best. You must have the courage to bear pain, disappointment, and heartbreak. You must learn how to face danger and understand fear, yet not be afraid. You establish your goal, and no matter what deters you along the way, in your every waking moment you must say to yourself, "I could do it.""

—*Betty Skelton, first lady of aerobatics*

Taking advantage of a modern phone system in a modern country that speaks a language I can understand, I dial ICU this morning to see if I can talk to Mama. Daddy maintains that I still can't speak to her but that she should be moving out of ICU and into a regular hospital room soon. Thank

goodness for this small step of progress. I find out later that
Daddy is stalling; Mama is unable to utter comprehensible
words, a side-effect from the stroke.

Still desperate for a better solution than the options available to me, I further investigate the possibility of going home
to see Mama. The travel agent is able to reduce the price of
the ticket to US $3,200, a fair value for the distance and con-
sidering the short notice. I bring it up to Jay.

"The travel agent has given me a price of $3,200 for a
round-trip ticket home," I mention.

Jay doesn't take the news well. "Are you still thinking
about going back?"

"Yes," I inform him. "My mother is still sick, isn't she?
The current schedule doesn't have us back for over two
weeks," I tell him. "That's a long time to be gone when my
mother is sick and my dad is alone trying to handle everything." My dad is 71.

He panics. "I don't think you'll come back," he admits.

After a pause, I say, "Can we cut some days out of the
schedule?"

He thinks about it.

After more discussion and with much hesitation, Jay con-
cedes, agreeing to accelerate the schedule so we can get back
earlier. But by now, there isn't much left to accelerate. We
have five destinations remaining before reaching Dallas:
Papua New Guinea, the Solomon Islands, Kiribatis, Hawaii,
and San Francisco. Jay consents to squeezing two days out
of the itinerary. It will still take us two weeks to get home.
But this alternative is better than abandoning the project,
which I don't want to do, especially this late in the flight and
after all we've come through successfully. I want to see this
flight through until the end. This is what I committed to, and
this is what I should do. My family will have to carry on

without me for a little while longer. I don't like that, but to accelerate the schedule any more would compromise crew rest, an unnecessarily dangerous risk.

I fax Sharon a tentative new schedule since all our permit dates will have to be modified:

	Depart	Arrive
YPDN - AYPY	8 SEP 2300Z*	9 SEP 0300Z (to Papua New Guinea)
AYPY - AGGH	10 SEP 0100Z	10 SEP 0500Z (to Solomons)
AGGH - NGTA	13 SEP 2200Z	14 SEP 0400Z (to Kiribatis)
NGTA - PHNL	15 SEP 2100Z	TBA (to Hawaii)

* The Z stands for Zulu time or GMT: Greenwich Mean Time

I also fax Mom a greeting:

> Hi Mom!
> We have made it to Darwin, Australia one day early. We are looking at accelerating the schedule but won't know anything for a few more hours.
> Everyone is extremely friendly here - this part of Australia is less populated and reminds me of Alaska people (but not the climate).
> I hear you will be leaving ICU soon. That's good news. Jay says you might have a sore throat from the tubes. Hope it's not too miserable for you. It sounds like you're well on your way to recovery.
> The weather is pretty and hot as it has been for much of the trip. Jay will be able to get the plane's oil changed and a belt tightened - the a/c belt keeps coming loose. There's actually someone in this country that we can trust to do the maintenance right.
> Today we'll do business (faxes, permits, maintenance) and tomorrow we'll go to a park probably for sightseeing.
> Take care -
> Love,
> Sandi

Jay rents a car, drives to the airport, and arranges with Trevor of Phoenix Aviation to perform badly needed maintenance on the Malibu. It needs an overdue 50-hour check and an oil change. Trevor inspects the air conditioning system and discovers that the air conditioning belt pulley is dislodged and rubbing against the pressurization mechanism. A bit more slippage and it would have damaged the plane, causing a dangerous situation for Jay and me. It's lucky it was caught in time; it could have been a real catastrophe if we'd taken even one more flight. I feel a huge relief. Trevor patches it so no further damage will happen, but he is unable to repair the air conditioning, so we'll have to carry on without it for the remainder of the trip. Jay schedules the fuel company to fill the airplane tomorrow morning.

I have tons of errands to do today. By now, I am efficient at these tasks and can get a lot done in a short amount of time. Before I start out, I ask the desk clerk at the hotel where I might find the places I need, and I mark them on the map. Then I plan my walking route. In no time, I change money, trek to the post office to mail back souvenirs I've collected, shop for more souvenirs, buy groceries so we can have some snacks in the room, and book a tour for tomorrow to see the Northern Territory.

The streets of Darwin are wide and clean. Most people get around in cars, but some walk; maybe these are other tourists. The people are friendly and helpful. Darwin reminds me of a small Texas town out in the country. No one is in a hurry here, except perhaps me.

Later I join Jay and we eat at a place called Hog's Breath Café. The restaurant's logo is a big-snouted pink pig holding a knife and a fork in each front foot. Its specialty is steak, but since Jay and I are vegetarians, we eat fish, potatoes, and salad.

In the morning, we rise before dawn to meet the tour bus at 6:30 for a "Kakadu Royale" tour. Barry is a one-man show: he is the tour driver, guide, and owner. Eight of us tourists ride in the air-conditioned bus on modern highways to visit Kakadu National Park and other Northern Australia sights, such as termite mounds and roadside restaurants. The termite mound is a sandy-colored rock-like structure that rises in a column shape from the ground. I take a picture of Jay next to one that's about 12 feet wide and 30 feet tall. Jay looks dwarfed next to it. There's no sign of termites; either they're inside resting or the colony has moved, leaving the mound empty.

The park contains aboriginal rock paintings, many of which were painted in 1967 by an elder called Barramundi Charlie, at a site called Ubirr. Charlie was the last remaining elder in the area because of problems with the way he initiated his protégés. When an initiate undertakes his vows, he is cut on his chest and ashes are rubbed in the wound to cause scarring. But Charlie's incisions sliced too deeply and his initiates died. The rest were frightened away. What a way to end a legacy of people, I think to myself. We "bushwalk" - as Australians call walking in the wild - among the rock formations and paintings as the sun heats up the day. It's quiet except for the occasional bird call and the muffled voices of tourists talking among themselves. I find the paintings primitive, raw, and fascinating. The white, brown, and red strokes are painted and etched on the multi-colored rocks. They depict the native's social, physical, and environmental aspects of life. Aboriginal life must have been so much simpler in these earlier times. It's no wonder in today's complexities that we get our priorities all out of whack all the time.

Many of the roads have no speed limit, indicated by a

sign with a red circle that has a slash through it. The roads are in good shape construction-wise, and flat for miles. Huge, long truck trailers blast down the highway at full speed, passing our bus. Many trucks pull two and three trailers at one time, swaying and see-sawing behind their cabs. It's a little nerve-wracking to be passed by one of these mighty rigs. The people of Australia strike me as a hardworking, fun-loving bunch. Barry, our guide, tells us what N. T. stands for: Northern Territory, not today, not tomorrow, not Tuesday, not Thursday, not tonight, no troubles.

Jay seems to be back to his usual self and enjoying the tour. In the afternoon, egrets, jabirus, pelicans, kingfishers, and magpie geese share the river with us during a cruise. The jabiru is an elegant long-legged, long-necked, and long-beaked water bird with a black and white body and a black head. The egrets are similar with an all-white coloring. An occasional bird call, a splash, and the guide's voice are all that we hear in this peaceful setting. Crocodiles, the world's largest reptiles, glide through the river, not making a noise, right next to our boat. The carnivores can hold their breath under water for an hour by slowing their heart rate down to two to three beats per minute. I think I might be holding my breath too as I am their prey. They can move from complete stillness to amazing speed in no time and have probably seen you long before you've seen them due to their ability to camouflage themselves. Sunlight spills sparkles onto the South Alligator River, which was misnamed by the Yanks, according to Barry. There are no alligators here, only crocs, he says. Crocodiles' ancestors date back to the days of dinosaurs. Our guide warns us not to put our hands outside of the boat, as if we need a warning.

Except for the endemic animals, this could be the swamps of Florida. I feel transported to another world in nature. It makes me serene for all of a few minutes. It is a pleasant diversion to flee from airplanes and hospital talk and become immersed in the unusual sights of the Northern Territory of Australia. Our boat cruise is over quickly, however. There's no more spare time, and tomorrow we're off to Port Moresby, Papua New Guinea.

In the morning, we dress in shorts to be as comfortable as possible for the hot weather. We hire a taxi to drive us to the airport. Jay struggles to file the flight plan over the phone while I visit the FAC office (Federal Airports Corporation) and move through Immigration. The plane is parked in General Aviation, a mile or two away, which requires us to take another taxi. We possess no key or password to get into the field, but there is a hole in the fence, so we crawl through to reach our plane. The plane hasn't been fueled, and there is no fuel truck in sight, so Jay searches for a company representative. The fuel worker doesn't have us on the list. We wait an hour for his service. It's 9:30 before we can depart.

Pointed east, we fly in heavy headwinds over Kakadu National Park, Arnhem Nation, the Great Barrier Reef, and the Coral Sea. Soaring a low 3,000 feet over the ground, we can spot the buildings, highways, trucks, and wildlife of the Northern Territory. Over Montana once, we were maintaining a similarly low altitude, and I teased Jay, "What kind of cow is that down there?" Having grown up on a farm, I knew the answer. He got a kick out of the fact that not only can you see cows, but you can tell what breed they are from the airplane.

A lady controller greets us on the radio over Papua New Guinea and asks us to change runways at the last minute. The runways are parallel, so Jay must engineer a sidestep. This is where the plane's nose remains pointed at the runways while moving to the side, in this case, the right. It's accomplished by finessing the rudders and keeping the yoke fairly still.

In flight school, there are numerous moves you learn to make on those first few flights. I was surprised when we practiced stalling the airplane on my very first flight. They will either scare you to death, build your confidence high, or do a little of both as it did for me. The instructor talked me through turns, dives, banks, climbs and, of course, takeoffs and landings. We had to recover the plane from unusual attitudes and keep our composure at the same time. All this was presented to me in a tiny two-seater during my first few hours of flying. It was difficult for me to keep from getting airsick, much less complete the maneuvers satisfactorily, but I managed to do it. I seem to become airsick more as a passenger than when I'm controlling the plane. It's a matter of keeping the brain focused on productive activity instead of how the body feels.

The Malibu alights on runway 14R and comes to rest after nearly seven hours.

On the ground, Lady Honia takes our General Declarations and says to come back in the morning to finish up. It's after 5:00 p.m., plus it's hot and muggy. We settle on the Gateway Hotel that is within walking distance of the airport and gobble the Australian-influenced buffet in the hotel restaurant. Jay and I eat a local whitefish, rice, and tropical fruit from the buffet. On TV, CNN broadcasts the news. I fax Daddy to let him know where we are.

In the morning, I return to the airport to complete the flight paperwork and to get visas. I'm impressed by this country's computer system: Immigration is fully automated, and it looks to me like every citizen who owns a passport is recorded in the computer. Jay and I are entered in as well.

Jay takes a morning run and explores the city by himself

via the local bus. I'm feeling like I want to be alone. I've already been to Rabaul, Papua New Guinea and had an extraordinary experience meeting a village of poor natives who lived by the river with homes built of World War II scraps. But I've read how much crime there is in Port Moresby and am a little afraid of the city. The tourist brochure warns about going out at night or into non-tourist areas. Statistically, Dallas is probably much more dangerous, but I find contentment on this day staying in the hotel room and nurturing myself as best as I can. With my mother's illness, the upcoming ocean flights, and being in a new place, it's all I can do to keep from curling up into a ball and staying there forever. My emotions are on redline right now, and my engine is about to overheat. Any more adventure would put me over the edge. I watch CNN in the hotel room and catch up on my diary entries. I write my mother a fax, but it doesn't go through. I telephone Daddy from a pay phone that eats my Guinea coins quickly and disconnects me prematurely. And I do my flight homework.

Every day before a flight, I fill in a flight planner for the next day's flight. This entails writing down the checkpoints along the way and calculating the distances. For example, from Papua New Guinea, waypoint AYPY, to the Solomons, waypoint AGGH, there are several checkpoints in between: DOMARA, GNY (GURNEY), GUVOG, REDOX, NIPOK (AGGG), IDSEK, and HN. I write each of these on a separate line on the planner and calculate the nautical miles between each one. Sometimes these waypoints are associated with an airport; others are simply geographical points on the route. I fill in the compass heading, the length en route, how many hours of fuel we need, and two alternate airports. The paper preparation is a backup to the other navigational aids. It also familiarizes us with the route. Homework done, I read the news.

The local news is interesting and curious, with rugby finals and an uprising in Bouganville Island. Apparently the government refused to pay for something and the landowners shut a business down. The police then came in and were killed, so there is a battle there now.

I spot men in the hotel parking lot dressed in colorful native costumes complete with grass skirts. They are not part of a tourist dance, I discover; they are celebrating their rugby team, the West Highlanders. They cheer and chant a *singsing* before they leave on a bus.

On September 16th, in less than a week, the country will celebrate its 20th anniversary of independence. Papua New Guinea's history is both very old and very recent. Fifty thousand years ago, the first humans from Asia crossed the Indonesian archipelago to find the rich islands of Papua New Guinea. The scenery includes mountains, tropical forests, steaming volcanoes, low lying swamps, and coral atolls. In 1512, Portuguese sailors named the island "Ilhas dos Papuas," or Islands of the Fuzzy Hairs." In 1545, the Spanish named the islands "New Guinea." In 1975 when the island declared its independence, it became Papua New Guinea, or PNG for short. PNG probably has had the least international influence on its culture, leaving some of its original cultures more intact than any others in the world. Eight hundred languages are still spoken in 200 cultures around PNG. English is spoken for business and government, and Pidgin and Police Motu are also widely spoken.

Jay returns after dark. "You should have come," he says.

"I had a good day," I reply. "I'm glad you did too."

"I don't understand why you stay in the hotel room," he says gently.

"I can't take as much adventure as you," I admit.

I don't think Jay gets it, but that's OK for now.

The flight to the Solomon Islands won't take too long, so we sleep in and leave the hotel at 7:15 a.m. I file the flight plan and retrieve the weather report, which is very sophisticated-looking. Packaged in a nice folder, the reports are in color. We clear Customs with help from an employee named Konio who stamps our passports. At the plane, a gentleman requests that we complete departure cards.

We fly over the island's mountainous forested peninsula, past the southern islands, and over the Solomon Sea. Although our ocean flying has started again, we won't have to use the auxiliary gas tank until we leave the Kiribati Islands. Halfway through the flight, rain showers and cumulus buildups challenge our path for an hour or so. As we approach Guadalcanal Island in the Solomon chain, the showers and clouds thin out. I feel better today and am anxious to see this country. We land in VFR (Visual Flight Rules) conditions and are again greeted by a man who hands Jay a spray can through his cockpit opening. Jay sprays the plane and I hold my breath again.

14

11 September, 1995
Honiara, Guadalcanal,
Solomon Islands

*"Courage is the price that life extracts
for granting peace.
The soul that knows it not, knows no
release from little things.
Knows not the livid loneliness of fear,
Nor mountain heights, where bitter joy
can hear
The sound of wings."*

—*Amelia Earhart*

*T*he first thing I need when I step out of the plane in this
sunny tropical paradise is something to drink. I am parched,
as I often am after a flight. I find a Fanta inside the terminal
building and slam it down. The airport is small and has a
countryside feel to it, with small buildings and hangars that

look a little like barns.

A mid-afternoon landing gives us some leisure time to arrange for fueling, clear Immigration and Customs, and chat with the mechanics hanging around the airport. Using the phone at the Solomon Airlines maintenance hangar, I book a hotel room. I have some Papua New Guinea *kinas* left, and it is an adventure converting them to Solomon Islands dollars. We all get confused on whether to multiply or divide the exchange rate.

I visit the briefing office, file a flight plan for our flight to Kiribati Islands, and order a weather report. Jay seems to be giving me more and more flying responsibilities as the trip progresses. The radio controller of the flight service station allows me to see how he tracks the planes with his equipment. These airport employees are by far the friendliest I have ever met. I notice a red splotch in the trash can. From my 1989 Papua New Guinea visit, I recognize this as betelnut but I don't say anything. Betelnut is something you can chew that will clean your teeth and give you a buzz at the same time. The only problem is it turns your whole mouth red while you chew it.

Late afternoon, Jay and I take a taxi to the Solomon Kitano Mendana Hotel. The hotel has recently undergone a Solomon $10 million facelift. The lobby is expansive and open with a long reception desk on one side. Fresh air blows through the lobby, unobstructed by doors or gates. The vaulted ceiling is made of rich wood, and thick wooden beams support the structure. The rooms are fresh and tropical with flowered fabric and blond furniture. I quickly walk around town as the shops close for the day. At dinner, we devour a fancy French feast, a fish and cheese dish in cream *veloute* sauce and a chocolate mousse to finish it off, in the hotel's restaurant. It's a romantic setting in paradise, an evening to be savored.

The next morning, we look for a tour. One tour company has its hands full with 40 Japanese, and another company doesn't have the tour we want. Jay and I look a little forlorn and lost near the reception desk. The hotel clerk suggests that we try a local guide named Mike. We take the bait. Mike just happens to be standing in the lobby and is quite friendly.

Mike hires a taxi; we climb in, and we drive to several fascinating war sites. On the way, he tells us a little about the history and the people. The capital Honiara takes its name from the native description of its site: *"naho ni ara,"* which means "facing the east and southeast winds." The people are 97 percent Christian and three percent worship their ancestral religion. Education is only required in the large cities and only until grades six or seven. If a woman wears a flower on her right side, it means she is married. On her left, she is available. If it's on top, she is desperate.

The Solomon Islands have a long history. The first inhabitants date back 30,000 years, but it was around 4,000 BCE when people with knowledge of sailing and agriculture settled here. The main island, Guadalcanal, was settled by Melanesians. New arrivals, Polynesians and Lapita people, settled in the outlying islands. In 1567, the Spanish in Peru sent an explorer, Don Alvaro de Mendaña y Neyra, to locate the islands. When he returned in 1568, his talk glorified the islands and they came to be called the islands of King Solomon. But the Solomon Islands were never accurately placed on any map, and it wasn't until 1767 that the British stumbled upon them. Unfortunately the Brits brought their diseases and thieving ways. To survive, the islanders learned to murder anyone who was white. The Solomons gained a reputation as a place even the missionaries avoided. In the

19th century, Britain colonized the islands, and during World War II the Japanese captured the westernmost islands. Some of the bloodiest fighting of the war between Americans and Japanese occurred here. In 1978, the Solomons gained their independence from Britain.

In 1942, the United States chose the island of Guadalcanal for their first major invasion of a Japanese-held island and it became a turning point in the war. On August 7, 1942, 16,000 troops invaded the island and Operation Watchtower was begun. The Japanese had started building an airstrip there which later became Henderson Field, now an international airport. After more than six months and nine major naval battles, the US declared Guadalcanal secure. The Japanese lost 24,000 men and the US lost 6,000. Sixty-seven ships were sunk in the nearby Pacific waters.

Mike stops and picks some pawpaw fruit on the roadside for us. It looks similar to a banana and tastes like a banana and vanilla custard blended together. He shows us battle sites, a memorial, and a hospital. He tells a heart-wrenching story of a man who came to the islands to visit the hospital where he lost his leg. Mike took him to the place where the operating theater (surgery room) stood, and the man recounted what that day was like. He tells this story so sincerely that I don't think I'll ever forget this moment. We climb down into a tunnel that was a headquarters, and see well-preserved equipment hidden away in camouflaged bunkers. He drives us to Alligator Creek, the site of the Battle of Tenaru. He tells us the story of how American Navajo Indians used their language as a code that the Germans or Japanese couldn't break. A 2002 movie, *Windtalkers*, documented the Navajos' important contribution in the war.

We visit the Red Beach. Mike tells us of a typhoon in 1986

that destroyed the rice fields. He says they now get a lot of their rice from Australia. It is currently the dry season, which will last until November. Finally, we visit a clam farm, the Coastal Aquaculture Center, where I learn more than I possibly can remember about giant clams. The clams were being rotated among settlement tanks, cages on racks, and nurseries, so we have a chance to view hundreds of them. Mike is a delight to be with, and the entire day is enjoyable and fascinating. Jay loves the historical sights.

After the tour, I wander around on my own for a while, visiting a cultural arts center, a museum and some shops that are near the hotel. I see several houses in the native style. One has totem poles to support the upside-down V-shaped thatched roof. Another has thatched walls and a roof and still another is round. The houses are built with coca leaves and bush timbers and are situated on hills where the breeze keeps the mosquitoes away. There are no other explanations about these houses, but they are interesting to look at anyway. I don't find too many books or t-shirts, which are the types of souvenirs I like. I love that this place is not commercialized at all. There is no McDonald's here. There is no commercial television. Even the Travel Fact File brochure says that the Solomon Islands are for people who can do without TV and McDonald's for a couple of weeks. Instead of man-made attractions, the islands rely on their natural resources: beautiful rainforests, mountains, volcanoes, waterfalls, beaches, and lagoons, to name just a few. For dinner, we munch a Japanese entrée with lobster in the hotel's Capitana Restaurant.

I make my phone call back home. I have become an expert at international calling. There's no change in Mama, says Daddy. I wince, wishing she would get better.

We've settled into a routine: arrive in a new place, get the airport paperwork completed, sightsee the following day, then leave for the next place. This gives us one day of crew rest in between the flights and gets me home quicker to see my ailing mother. I'm trying to be less anxious on this part of the trip; I've done everything I can do to get home sooner. But it's not the rational part that is challenging; it's the emotional part that's a challenge for me.

In the morning, it's another flying day. Jay and I taxi to the airport, obtain a weather report, and wait for Customs to arrive. The Customs officers, once they arrive, are very speedy and we take off after loading the plane.

Before we left on this trip, we had to purchase all of the aviation publications that covered our planned route. This included an international flight information manual, the charts for the sections of the skies we needed, the IFR (instrument flight rules) supplements, and the approach plates for all the airports in the region. Approach plates list detailed airport information, including taxiways, acceptable landing patterns, and communication protocols with airport tower personnel. Before landing, air traffic controllers at a center must transfer control of an airplane to the airport tower, which clears the plane to land. This procedure is usually initiated five to ten miles from the airport. We need two suitcases just to hold all this paperwork. We're missing a chart we need for today but we do have the waypoints written down.

Over the Solomons, we dodge clouds, including one that alarms me because of its sudden turbulence. I fly the airplane for most of today in partly cloudy conditions. I also make the radio calls. I stay in touch with Honiara for quite a while, until I fly out of radio reach. Over Nauru the radio breaks up, and we only receive Tarawa, our destination, at the very end of the flight. Tarawa is an island in the Kiribatis chain, 1,000 miles northeast of the Solomons, and 2,000 miles southwest of Hawaii. Just barely north of the Equator, it's the most remote place we'll visit on this trip, and I'm really looking forward to seeing what secrets the country holds.

The island of Tarawa is the flattest I've ever seen and it's shaped in a V. Tropical vegetation covers the island except at the edges, where a tiny strip of white sand lines the island's perimeter. From the air, you can see the outline of shallow submerged land that surrounds the islands. The island chain is a coral atoll surrounded by many reefs. Boats must run aground all the time, I think. The highest point on any of the islands in this chain is about 200 feet. Turquoise waters reach out for miles in every direction. The airport is located at the intersection of the two lines in the letter V. We land and I taxi the plane to parking. We clear Agriculture's spray can, Customs, and Immigration. The people of Kiribati are courteous and welcoming. Jay sees to refueling the plane. Kiribati offers the green-tinted, higher-lead 100/130 octane fuel that is illegal in the United States, and the plane sucks in 682 liters as we fill the auxiliary tank for the first time since Delhi. We'll need it on the 2,000-mile trip to Hawaii.

There's only one tourist-class hotel in Tarawa: the Otintaai. In the hot and humid mid-afternoon, we take a bus there and check in. The bus is a public bus that runs up and down the one road all day long. The driver stops if he sees someone by the side of the road so the passengers can board, and he also stops when someone wants to get off. Otherwise, there are no regular stops.

The lady at the hotel desk is incredibly helpful. The people of Kiribati value characteristics such as kindness, bravery, and mercy. Family is important to them, and every birth, marriage, and death is a reason to gather. The Kiribatis take stock of who attends these events, because favors will be due in the future. The people dress informally and for the weather here. Women wear a shirt and skirt or shorts. Men wear pants and a shirt. They may or may not match. Children wear only a skirt or shorts. There's probably not a lot of choice of fabrics and ready-to-wear that comes this way. About 38,500 people live on this island.

Jay begins exploring while I do laundry and read what the guidebook says about this incredibly remote place. In the evening, we eat at the only place around: the hotel restaurant, which serves a delicious local reef fish. The setting is casual yet romantic. We're both in a grand mood.

I wake up to a cold shower. In such a remote place, you can't be too picky about luxuries like hot water. Jay has one thing on his mind as usual: airplane business. He calls his insurance company. As soon as we cross the International Date Line tomorrow, his plane will be insured again. I take advantage of the friendly, helpful staff at the hotel desk and send my parents a fax.

> Hi Mom and Dad,
> We are in Tarawa, Republic of Kiribati now. Staying at Otintaai Hotel Room 29. You can call country code 686 local # 28020. 011 68628020 room 29 I think. We'll be leaving at 2:00 p.m. on September 14 your time. I'll be glad when we cross the date line - it took me 30 minutes to figure out when to call and fax this. The fax in Papua New Guinea didn't go through, I didn't try in the Solomons.
> Hope you're doing well. Glad to see you're in a regular room and out of ICU. Hope to talk to you soon. The people of these islands just get nicer and nicer.
> Love,
> Sandi

After our business, Angie, our tour guide who was arranged by the hotel, is ready to take us on an excursion of Tarawa. Angie tells us of the importance of the family unit. The head of the household represents the other members in any business and governmental matters. Each village contains a meeting house, which is the social center of the community. We visit an ancestral shrine and a rock where there is an ancient giant footprint which has been made into an altar. Our driver leaves a stick of tobacco in each place as an offering. Women cannot visit the shrine while having their period. One local woman who made this mistake fell ill and had to go to the hospital. A few elders still practice magic in the village. We also visit a handicrafts shop, full of tightly woven baskets made of palms and shells. The US Army built a school here last year, and the Japanese built a causeway here in 1989. Mormon, Baha'i, and Catholic churches offer worship here. The beach displays two huge rusted Japanese guns, pointing out to sea at an invisible enemy. Two small boys climb on top of them and make machine gun sounds with their voices.

There is no television to speak of on this island. The people entertain themselves the old-fashioned way, by telling stories. Angie tells how important music is and that all Kiribati people can sing. Children sing while playing, grandparents sing to their grandchildren, teens sing after school, and adults sing while working or partying.

On this island, the people are Micronesians. Micronesia is a geographical designation for the Pacific islands to the north and east of Papua New Guinea. The territory stretches from the Philippines to the Hawaiian Islands. In the Solomon Islands, the people are Melanesians. Melanesia comprises the islands east and south of Papua New Guinea, all the way to Fiji. In Hawaii, the people are Polynesians.

The difference among these Pacific Islanders is geographical and cultural. The inhabitants have nice, genuine smiles here. The guide book says the people are shy.

It's destinations like the Kiribatis that make me so passionate about traveling. To be able to see such a different lifestyle and different people is beyond fascinating to me. It might be natural to constantly judge a new culture when we hear about it or see it. But if you can develop your skills to remove that instinctive judgment we all have, you'll find the treasure.

People are valued much more than time on this island. You will never hear a Kiribati who is in the middle of an important conversation say, "I have to go now." Kiribatis value their land, canoes, and houses as well, but these are the only material possessions they care about. They value so highly their skills and knowledge that they consider them secrets, not to be given away. They have a strong pride to do the right thing where others are concerned. Singing all the time, they are happy people. They seem to have less greed than other peoples, and I wish that trait could be transported to the US.

A fascinating practice of the Kiribati people concerns when a girl reaches puberty, called *te katekateka*. She is seated in the meeting house or at a special family hut. Her aunts provide her with skirts made of chewed coconut leaves to absorb the menstrual flow. The girl must eat only dry coconut and water for three days. Following the end of her first menstruation, there is a huge feast where relatives celebrate.

Jay makes the flight arrangements for tomorrow, and I call my dad to see how Mama is doing. She is stable. Kid is still by my dad's side, all 82 years young of her.

Tomorrow, the risky over-water flying begins again. In

the next two flights, we need to cover over 2,000 miles each, with flight times of greater than 11 hours each.

At 6:30 a.m., we leave the Otintaai Hotel in the hotel's van and drive to the airport. The van driver takes us right up to the plane. I walk back to the airport offices to see if anyone is home. No one is. We have to wait for the Customs and Immigration officer to arrive before we can leave. At 7:10, he does, and we're off.

Our ground speed as we climb is very poor this flight, only 120 knots. The headwind is not bad, less than 15 knots. As we go higher, our speed seems to improve. We stop the climb frequently, leveling off, then later resume the climb. We eventually make it to 190 knots, which is above average.

About four hours into the flight, we cross north of Howland Island, the island that Amelia was aiming for when she went missing. Howland Island is roughly 600 miles east of Tarawa. I stare down into the ocean below us. It was Amelia's husband who came up with the idea of her landing on Howland Island. In May 1936, the US government gained control of Howland as well as two other nearby islands, Jarvis and Baker. They were able to arrange for the government to build a scratch-grade runway on the tiny sand bar in the Pacific.

I'm not sure why Amelia didn't nix the plans. She didn't even plan for a backup island. There were plenty of islands between Lae, Papua New Guinea and Howland Island, including the outer islands of Papua New Guinea, The Solomon Islands, Nauru, Kiribati Islands, Marshall Islands, and Fiji and the Cook Islands. The latter two choices would have taken her decidedly south, but still in range of Hawaii. All of these chains had numerous islands, even though most of them wouldn't have had landing strips in the 1930s.

To compound things, she left Lae at 10:22 a.m., with an

ETA of 6:15 a.m. over Howland. At the Equator, sunrise is at 6:00 a.m. Why would she plan the last part of her flight in the dark when she couldn't see the land under her? Shortly after sunrise, the sun would still be so low in the sky that even if the island was directly below her, she might not have seen it because of the glare.

Many more poor decisions were made by Amelia or on her behalf. Her husband decided to paint the rudder in Purdue's colors because it had donated money and was a sponsor of the trip. This resulted in a plane that was painted black and a dull gold, rather than a vibrant life-saving emergency color like orange. In aviation, you just can't make that many mistakes and get away with your life.

From roughly 6:00 a.m. to 8:00 a.m., the Navy could hear Amelia's radio messages but she could not hear the Navy. She didn't stay on the transmission long enough for them to get a fix on her. She only radioed them her position once. It was probably incorrect anyway.

Amelia Earhart and her navigator, Fred Noonan, were the subjects of the most extensive mass rescue attempt for a single lost plane in history. Over 16 days, 4,000 men searched 250,000 square miles of the Pacific in 10 ships and 65 planes with no results. Although the mystery of her disappearance is unsolved today, the logical conclusion is that she ran out of gas. She likely ditched in the Pacific and drowned as the plane sunk into the 13,000-feet deep waters.

Closer to Hawaii, Honolulu Center is clear when they answer our calls. Several times there is no answer. Sunset falls about ten hours into our flight, a few hours before we are scheduled to reach Hawaii. The dark orange glow of the sun consumes half of the horizon behind us, ending in blackness in my peripheral vision on the sides of the plane. The big dipper lies on the horizon to the north.

As we fly toward Honolulu, just for fun and a little history trivia, we copy the Japanese's way of navigating just before their attack on Pearl Harbor. Jay tunes in an AM radio station from Hawaii on the automatic direction finder. The needle automatically points to the station.

On approach, Jay talks with the controller who is speaking very conversationally for a change. "Where are you coming in from tonight?" he asks.

Jay answers enthusiastically, "We're traveling eastbound from Dallas, Texas to Dallas, Texas."

A commercial pilot chimes in, "Is that the Concord?"

"No," the controller says matter-of-factly. "It's a Piper Malibu."

We all have a good laugh at that one.

Just before landing, my headset fails; I can't hear Jay's voice and he can't hear me, but I can hear the VHF over the speaker. The turbine inlet temperature gauge acts up. Even with these equipment failures, I have to feel thankful; we haven't had nearly the problems on the last half of this trip that we had on the first part, and that's a wonderful feeling. The long hours on this leg of the journey take their toll on Jay and me; we're both dog tired the last few hours of this flight.

Jay lands in the dark and taxies to an FBO which is closed. FBO stands for Fixed-Base Operator, a company that provides general aviation pilots and crew access to fuel, parking, maintenance services, flight planning, weather forecasts, and even shower facilities at airports. We pull up in front of a maintenance facility working on Mahalo Airline planes. A Customs agent approaches us.

"Do you have Prior Landing Rights permission?" the officer asks Jay. We're not on his list. It's probably fortunate we didn't get shot down.

Jay wearily says he tried to make the call from the

Solomon Islands but was unable to get through. The officer seems satisfied, and he asks for lots of paperwork: a certificate of airworthiness, proof of insurance, Jay's pilot's license, and General Declarations. Jay's US Customs decal has expired, and he buys a new one for $25 from the agent. Officers from Agriculture and Immigration join us, asking for a General Declaration form. A man from the airport also visits to collect parking and landing fees. He shows us where to park and even gives us a ride to a hotel.

After we settle in, we find a fast food restaurant. Right after dinner, walking the streets, I see a sight familiar in the US: a homeless bag lady. Although beggars are common in other countries, I haven't noticed any on our trip. After a dose of Jay Leno, we sleep for the first time in three months on a bed in our own country.

When we wake up, we get to do September 15th all over again since we crossed the International Date Line during flight.

September 15, 1995
Honolulu, Hawaii, USA

"Whatever you can do or dream you can, begin it. Boldness has genius, power and magic in it."

—*Goethe*

*M*ama takes a turn for the worse and has an irregular heartbeat on top of all her other problems. I feel overwhelmingly helpless and have no idea how I can help. When I call my dad, he says to call back later. The doctors will be giving Mama an echocardiogram of sorts this morning, so I should call back when they know the results. It seems the closer I get, the worse Mama is doing. I am completely miserable thinking about my mom lying in a hospital bed fighting for her life. Now in Hawaii, I am closer to being able to reach her, but I'm still not able to be by her side. We have only one more long, over-water flight left. I feel very impatient; it's all I can do to see this trip through. The AT&T operator notifies

me that I am over my credit limit. I tell her my circumstances, almost sobbing, and she gives me a bigger credit
limit.

Jay rents a sedan so we can run errands and sightsee
today. He drives to the airport and fixes my headset, which
I am ecstatic about. I did not like the feeling of not being able
to hear during those final few minutes of the last flight. It
was too scary to be in the dark about what's happening
onboard. We swap hotels to get a non-smoking room for the
night at a Holiday Inn. We stop at McDonald's and devour
fish sandwiches and fries. The familiar tastes and smells of
grease and burgers leaves me with a feeling that we're closer
to home. We drive through the city streets of Oahu to
Honolulu Harbor to see the Maritime Museum. Palm trees
tower over the cement structures of a typical small US city.
The museum is located at Pier Seven next to the blue waters
of the harbor. Inside the painted blue, gray, and turquoise
building are several memorable highlights. The island's history of Polynesian travelers and whalers is explained in
exhibits, text, and pictures. The skeleton of a humongous
humpback whale is suspended in air and takes up a gigantic
room and both stories of the building. The skull itself is 750
pounds and 12 feet, and the entire skeleton is made up of 159
bones. The whale even has a name: *Leiiwi*, which means "Lei
of the cherished bones."

In other exhibits, the history of surfing is explained, as is
whaling. Canoe racing is also described, and there is a long
beautiful wooden canoe that hangs from the ceiling.
Outside the museum, the *Falls of Clyde* is available for boarding. At 165 feet in length and over a thousand tons, it's a
four-masted, fully-rigged ship built in 1878 used in the sugar
trade and later to haul petroleum. It's the only one left of its
kind.

Next door to the USS Arizona Memorial Visitor Center is the USS Bowfin Submarine Museum and Park, which is made up of a museum, a memorial, and an actual submarine you can explore. The museum contains the history of submarines. Did you know the first one dates back to 1776? We embark the cramped and equipment-filled quarters of the USS Bowfin, nicknamed the Pearl Harbor Avenger because she sank 44 enemy ships while in service. The Waterfront Memorial honors the 52 subs and 3,500 men lost in World War II. A tall flag waves in the wind, silently honoring the fallen.

As interesting as these sights are, my heart is just not into it today. I take a break from history to find out how my mom is doing in the present. Daddy says Mama has a blood clot in her heart. She will take a blood thinning agent to try to dissolve it. It's not fair that she should have so many problems all at once. It's a good thing she is a fighter. I wish I were by her side right now. I'm so ready to get back to the mainland, but we have several days planned here in Hawaii.

Late afternoon, we drive to Diamond Head, the famous volcanic crater at the end of Waikiki that overlooks the Pacific. The volcano has been dormant for centuries and the crater is well-formed at 3,520 feet in diameter with a 760-feet summit. There is no shade anywhere. We walk part of the paved Diamond Head trail to admire the view of Waikiki and the rest of Oahu. From this vantage point, you can see the rooftops dotting the tropical vegetation of the island. High-rise hotels line the crowded sandy Waikiki Beach. The Pacific waters reach for miles until they crest against the brown cliffs of Oahu. The sun beats down on all of this, making the blues, whites, and greens brighter than ever.

In the morning, I take the controls of the Malibu and fly from Honolulu to Hilo at a spectacularly low altitude - 500 feet - skirting the island coastline and soaking up the scenery filled with waterfalls, black sand beaches, mountain cliffs, and ocean waves. Jay, crazy with enthusiasm, gapes at the scenery out the window; he loves flying low. Alaska was the first time we flew low, copying the custom of pilots from that state. Since then, Jay flies low whenever he can get away with it. It's only a little scary for me because there isn't any room for error if something happens. We land at Hilo. It's the first time in months we don't have to clear Immigration. We eat at McDonald's (yes, again!).

Near the end of the trip, Jay is starting to splurge a little. We stay at Volcano House Hotel, a cluster of three red buildings in Volcano Park. A view from the dining room overlooks Kilauea Crater, but it's foggy so we can't see anything. We drive to the Chain of Craters Road, and walk a ways over black solidified lava to visit the freshest lava flow - from May 7, 1995 - and see the red glow under black crust. Steam rises where the lava meets the ocean. We can only see these things from a distance. The roads are blockaded, and policemen stand guard for public safety.

In the morning, I send Mama this fax:

> Hi Mom,
>
> Looks like I should be home in less than a week. On Tuesday, we'll fly to Oakland, CA. We have already done the hardest leg from Kiribati to Honolulu. The hardest part of this flight will be getting the agricultural clearance while we're still on the ground.
>
> Sounds like you're very busy, with lots to do, among therapists, doctors, and nurses.
>
> Today we're going to hike around the volcano and take a day of rest from flying. Yesterday the flight from Honolulu to Hilo was very beautiful but

it was over 100° in the cockpit. Up here at a little elevation, it's cooler.

Take care of yourself. I'll talk to you soon.

Love,

Sandi

Today we drive through Hawaii Volcanoes National Park, stopping to hike frequently. My favorite thing to do on vacations is to hike trails in our National Parks. We stroll along the easy half-mile of Devastation Trail and see the part of the park that was destroyed by an eruption in 1959. Many trees and plants have grown back, but there are still cinders everywhere. These look like small black pebbles. Many pieces of wood along the way look petrified. The trail ends at the Pu'u Pua'i Overlook where we see the Kilauea Iki Crater, a black sunken circle of barren land. I want to hike to the petroglyphs, so we find the trail leading to Pu'u Loa and walk not quite a mile. There are stick figures and fancy circles carved on the black rock. Their age is unknown, but historians do know it was considered a holy place by the original inhabitants.

The trip to the craters is the last of the sightseeing we'll do on this trip. For me, it has been a real struggle to try to enjoy sightseeing while thinking about my mom. In a way, I am relieved because I have been to so many countries and seen so many things that my excitement threshold is getting higher and higher. In other words, I can easily get burned out on tourist sights. With every new place I see, it gets harder and harder to impress me with new sights. But I'm also sad because these times were an incredible opportunity not fully embraced. Daily life back in Dallas won't be nearly as exciting and varied as it has been on this trip.

Finally, the day comes when we will take off for San

Francisco. This is the last challenging flight we have; the last over-water flight and the last flight where we will use the auxiliary fuel tank. The first thing we have to do is to meet with a representative from Agriculture to obtain a certificate. He arrives promptly at 8:15 a.m., and we are cleared.

Over the Pacific, the weather is exquisite, with bright sunshine and no clouds. There's a certain freedom to be felt in the air as you're soaring along with nothing underneath you. We make our position reports over the high frequency radio, stating our latitudes and longitudes. We use the frequency 128.95 that is designated as the official pilot-to-pilot communication channel to chat with a few airline pilots along the way. An Air Force plane trails us for a while.

I spot a black speck on the blue ocean below. It's a ship of some kind. Jay looks at it through his binoculars. It's a cargo ship, he says.

"It's a good time to test the handheld radio. I'll call the ship," Jay tells me. He calls the ship on a marine VHF channel 16. An officer of the ship answers. Jay tells him we're flying above him and testing our equipment. The officer acknowledges. It's probably not every day he gets a radio call from an airplane, but we are glad for the equipment check. Even though we're nearing the end of the trip, it's best not to let your guard down. Constantly checking and re-checking equipment will keep us alert, prepared, and hopefully alive.

I think about what we've accomplished these last few months. My flying skills have improved markedly. My knowledge of teamwork has always been strong, having worked in a Fortune 50 company, but this trip gave me a chance to be a team member when life and death were potentially on the line, something I haven't previously been a party to. There is little room for error; you have to do things right the first time. And although stressful, the opportunity gives you a chance to grow and stretch into the circumstances that arise.

I've learned a lot from visiting so many different cultures in such a short time frame. There is much we can learn from each one of them. The world could learn from Tanger about how people of varying religions live side by side in peace. From Djibouti, we could learn how to stop fearing scarcity. From the Thai people, we could learn fun and tolerance. From Bali, we could learn about politeness and beauty. From the Aussies, we could learn how to enjoy nature. From the Pacific Islanders, we could learn about what true friendship without greed looks like.

Toward the mainland, dusk catches up with us and an orange glow is replaced by millions of stars plus the glow of lights in San Francisco Bay. Over the bay, there are so many runways below; who knows which one is the right one? Jay uses the Instrument Landing System to guide our way, and we land after 11 hours and five minutes. It's a major milestone; we've crossed both oceans now, and all we have left is to get from San Francisco to Dallas, a flight we can do in our sleep. A Bonanza right behind us lands on the wrong runway: the right one instead of the left one. No damage is done, but it reinforces how easy it is to make a mistake. We park in front of an FBO, Kaiser Air. Jay kisses the ground, and we share a "Whoop" and a celebratory hug. A van takes us to a Motel 6, and we chow down at Denny's before sleeping.

In the morning, our moods are lighter and each of us calls everyone we know, letting them know we're back safe. We spend the day meeting with the Executive Director of the Seva Foundation, the nonprofit group that works with the eye hospital in Nepal. The following day, we make the final leg from San Francisco to Dallas. Thunderstorms plague us the entire way. It would be easy to become arrogant with all we've accomplished, slip up, and make a mistake, but we don't. In the worst weather of the trip, lightning, turbulence, and rain, we are diligent and careful with every task we perform in the cockpit. We land safely at Addison Airport, 86 days after starting our journey.

Upon parking, Jay is ecstatic. "I can't believe we pulled that off," he says.

I give myself a few moments to celebrate our success. I'm proud and humbled to be one of the few women in the world who has ever accomplished such a flight. I put aside all of my tensions and fears to cherish this moment.

"Thanks for the chance," I say sincerely and lovingly, looking Jay straight in the eye.

Jay nods in acknowledgement.

The biggest thing I learned on this trip is what it takes to be extraordinary. Extraordinary people continue to accomplish their dreams no matter what. If they don't feel like doing their dream that day, they accomplish something anyway. They push through the pain. They do extraordinary things whether they feel like it or not, because they are committed no matter what.

Extraordinary people realize that they will be presented with challenges that exist on an entirely new level. These challenges would never come up if they were trying to be ordinary. The challenges really help them to grow and become stronger for circumstances that will come up in the future.

Extraordinary people complete what they start out to do, no matter what gets in the way. They don't do it alone, however. They have the support of people around them. And with that, their level of mastery reaches the stars.

I learned that it takes even more passion to complete a trip like this than I expected. And that sometimes the personal sacrifices you have to make along the way hurt dearly.

Amelia's higher aspirations live on in many of us. There were two things she wanted: the first was for airline travel to flourish, and the second was for women to become prominent in aviation and to be able to make a contribution to the field without discrimination. There is still much to accomplish with Amelia's second aspiration.

16

September 21, 1995
Dallas, Texas, USA

"Sometimes I've believed as many as six impossible things before breakfast."

—Lewis Carroll, Alice in Wonderland

In 86 days, Jay and I flew the Malibu for 147:23 hours a distance of 25,303 nautical miles. We traveled to 19 countries and two geographically separate territories (Hawaii and the Azores), plus two others by land (Morocco and Gibraltar). We used 2,290 gallons of aviation gasoline and averaged 171.7 knots per hour, or 197.6 miles per hour. It's not a record; we're not the first to achieve this feat. But it was our dream, and we fulfilled it.

Now it's time for "real life." I make a beeline to the hospital to see my mother.

Epilogue

After teaching computer classes in Mombasa, I started a business in Dallas teaching people how to use computers and the Internet, a relatively new idea in late 1995. I also wrote books on technology, and my business was off to a great start. My mother overcame even more complications and eventually came home from the hospital. She was bedridden for the remaining years of her life and passed away in May 2000. I continued my passion for traveling, and in 2004 I visited my 100th country and joined the elite Travelers' Century Club.

In 1996, Jay Merten sold the Piper Malibu and purchased a Citation Jet. He continued his passion for flying and became a commercial pilot in 1998 for Atlantic Southeast Airways, a commuter airline owned by Delta. He now owns a black Ferrari which has more horsepower than the Malibu did, plus a 40-foot Pacific Seacraft yacht that is circumnavigating the Pacific as this book goes to print.

Although Jay and I stopped seeing each other as a couple in 1999, we remain friends to this day.

Sources

Donald M. Goldstein and Katherine V. Dillon, <u>Amelia: A Life of the Aviation Legend</u>, Brassey's, Washington, 1999.

Doris Rich, <u>Amelia Earhart: A Biography</u>, Smithsonian Institution Press, Washington, 1989.

National Transportation and Safety Board. www.ntsb.gov.

About the Author

Sandi Smith has written eight books, over 200 articles, and several seminars and courses. Her writing has won awards and has been published internationally.

In addition to her writing, Sandi is a frequent speaker at conferences and seminars and has presented her programs to thousands of people. A CPA, Sandi holds an MBA and spent over a decade as a project manager working in Fortune 100 IT shops. She is currently working on a Masters of Science in Applied Cognition and Neuroscience.

A member of the Travelers Century Club, Sandi has visited 101 countries, including a backpacking trip alone around the world. Her volunteer work in Kenya, Russia, and Nepal earned her the 1996 AWSCPA Public Service Award and the Baird Community Service Award in March 1996.

To find out more, visit her web site at:
http://www.followingamelia.com.

Bulk Orders

Interested in providing a copy of this book to all the members of a group? Employees of your corporation? Conference participants? Members of your association? Save big by ordering in bulk quantities! Please contact us at orders@followingamelia.com so we can provide you with a special quote for the quantity of books you need. We appreciate your business.

Feedback

We'd love to hear from you. Please let us know what you liked and didn't like about the book. What will you tell your friends about?

Send us an email at feedback@followingamelia.com.